An account of a boy born into poverty and extremely difficult circumstances, during a time of global war, and the resulting events, which would influence the rest of his life.

It also attempts to reflect his social beliefs in today's burgeoning climate of disparity and the worldwide greed-oriented society.

This book is dedicated to my dear departed wife, Gillian, who encouraged me and drove me on when I was ready to quit studying at college and who worked her fingers to the bone trying to help me.

They say that behind every man who succeeds, there is a woman.

Beyond a shadow of a doubt, Gillian was that woman.

Kenneth Roger Adams

Two Left Shoes

AUSTIN MACAULEY PUBLISHERS™
LONDON • CAMBRIDGE • NEW YORK • SHARJAH

Copyright © Kenneth Roger Adams 2024

The right of Kenneth Roger Adams to be identified as author of this work has been asserted by the author in accordance with sections 77 and 78 of the Copyright, Designs and Patents Act 1988.

All rights reserved. No part of this publication may be reproduced, stored in a retrieval system, or transmitted in any form or by any means, electronic, mechanical, photocopying, recording, or otherwise, without the prior permission of the publishers.

Any person who commits any unauthorised act in relation to this publication may be liable to criminal prosecution and civil claims for damages.

All of the events in this memoir are true to the best of author's memory. The views expressed in this memoir are solely those of the author.

A CIP catalogue record for this title is available from the British Library.

ISBN 9781035850143 (Paperback)
ISBN 9781035850150 (ePub e-book)

www.austinmacauley.co.uk

First Published 2024
Austin Macauley Publishers Ltd®
1 Canada Square
Canary Wharf
London
E14 5AA

Acknowledgement

1. My very esteemed, inspirational and valuable friend Sir Arthur C. Clarke, whom I believe to have been one of the greatest visionaries of our time.
2. Sir Arthur's brother Fred, who I always regarded as 'A gentleman of the old school'.
3. Mrs Valerie Ekanayake, wife of Hector, who ran Sir Arthur's SCUBA Diving School.
4. Mr Stefan Birckmann, the German man who revived the traditional Sri Lankan puppets which were instrumental in helping traumatised (tsunami victim children).
5. My French sister-in-law, Mrs Brigitte Adams, who accompanied me and Fred Clarke to Sri Lanka following the 2004 tsunami.
6. Nick Chipchase allowed me to use his photographs of 'old Taunton' including the one showing a little Girl standing next to a Tram.
7. Sarah Morris Armer has kindly given written permission to use the photo of children sitting on a doorstep and followed by her poem *'When I was just a little girl'* copyright 2018 and altered by me to read *'When I was just a little boy'*.

Table of Contents

Foreword	**12**
No Silver Spoon	**36**
Bless This House	**107**
The Long Tunnel of Adversity	**113**
'They'	**132**
Fear, Self and Money	**139**
Philanthropy	**142**
Gillian and Helen	**147**
Backwards Progress	**160**

The war, the boy, the lost island of his hometown and the journey to the lost island of Britain, which was once Great Britain.

From austerity to excess and the threat to our planet.

This book is dedicated to my dear departed wife, Gillian, who drove me on with her exceptionally kind encouragement when I was ready to quit studying at college and who worked her fingers to the bone trying to help me.

They say that behind every man who succeeds, there is a woman. Beyond a shadow of a doubt—Gillian was that woman.

Foreword

I felt compelled to write this book, but when I sat down and began writing it, I soon began to realise that other events, much earlier in my life, were inextricably bound-up within the story and that I would need to include some of them, so a lot of actual dates would be needed. I suspect that many writers have suddenly come to that same realisation.

The central theme was to have been the terrifying ordeal, which my wife and I, found ourselves subjected to when our decision to buy a piece of land and build our own house went horribly wrong, but my story began to develop into much more than that.

I began to realise that my life had developed along a path which somehow seemed pre-determined by the circumstances of the time, by my parent's situation and which over time, has made me believe that this world has developed over my lifetime in a way which could be much better than it is now.

The thing I now hope to project is the great disparity which has grown ever wider and the 'Greed Engine' which drives it.

With the house build, we found ourselves experiencing a 'living nightmare'. Although it is true to say that everyone will have good times and bad times during the course of their lives, it is not until you get a taste of the really bad that you come to realise the terrifying plight people can find themselves in. It is a situation which shows you what a real friend is. It is also an experience which humbles you and teaches you to have compassion.

I would certainly now say to anyone: "Never mock someone who is struggling against the odds, it could easily happen to you one day."

An account of what happened during 'The House-Build', will follow later in this book.

So now, this book also contains all sorts of issues which will, I hope, illustrate the enormous changes that have taken place in only seventy years or so.

Changes in attitudes, values, degree of prosperity or indeed poverty and things which were unacceptable then, which seem acceptable now. Changing values which will probably cause people of my own generation to reminisce and the modern generation to wonder and find it hard to believe. Regrettably, I have no children of my own and I am aware that some might think I am not qualified to comment on some of the issues I intend to mention.

Our story contains examples of poverty and prosperity, close friendship, great divides, love and hate, admiration and despise. I believe that in many ways it is a reflection of changing times and changing values and of the ways in which people respect or fail to respect each other.

It does now seem to me that since the birth of the greed-oriented society we now live in reared its ugly head, following the Margaret Thatcher era, things have slowly progressed to make things much better in some ways but

also worse in other ways for ordinary working people and for the planet we live on. This is now mainly intended to be what my story now aims to convey by telling what I have seen and attempting to show how we lived then and how so much is taken for granted nowadays and concern for how until now, our world's future is treated almost with contempt.

****

I am a Somerset man and was always very proud to be British. My grandfather fought in the First World War as a Sapper in the Royal Engineers.

I am also a Tauntonian and I am actually quite proud of that too.

Taunton was a place of great strategic importance, it is 'The gateway to the west'.

During the Civil War of the 1640s, the town sided with the Parliamentarians of Oliver Cromwell and its defence was ably led by Admiral Blake who withstood 3 Royalist Sieges until Oliver Cromwell sent a relieving force of his 'Ironsides' under the very able General Fairfax. They approached the town from the south and drove off the besiegers. It would appear that Taunton played an important part in that war because they 'tied-up' a large number of Royalist troops through three unsuccessful sieges, who could otherwise have been at Naseby, which was the decisive victory for the Parliamentarians.

Furthermore, Fairfax's troops pursued the Royalists from Taunton to Langport and routed them in the battle that followed there at Wagg Drove.

Taunton's Coat of Arms bears the word 'Defendamus', which means 'we shall defend' and it features a peacock. Taunton Town Football Club are nicknamed 'The Peacocks'. They play in The National League.

Someone at the time (or later), wrote the following:

>The eleventh of May was a joyous day,
>When Taunton got relief;
>Which turned our sorrows into joy,
>And spared us of our grief.
>Long time did Goring lie encamped
>Against fair Taunton town;
>He made a vow to starve us out,
>And batter our castle down.
>Our beer was eighteen-pence per quart,
>As for a truth was told,
>And butter eighteen-pence per pound
>To Christians, there was sold.
>The cavaliers dispersed with fear,
>And forced were to run,
>On the eleventh of May, by break of day;
>Ere rising of the sun.
>Let Taunton men be mindful then,
>In keeping of this day;
>We'll give God praise with joy always,
>Upon the eleventh of May.

(Following the second Royalist Siege, 1645)—Anon.

On 1 May 1886, Taunton was the first town in the south-west to be permanently lit by electric street lights. They were carbon arc lamps.

Taunton is the county town of Somerset and its county hall is situated only a few minutes' walk from the town centre along Corporation Street.

On an elevated piece of ground behind the county hall stands the Shire Hall, a magnificent gothic building which is the home of Taunton Crown Court.

The foundation stone for this building was laid in 1855, together with a bottle containing coins and parchment documents. The building work was completed in 1858.

Old picture of Shire Hall

****

Across the road from the front of the Shire Hall stands the old Police Station on the corner of Burton Place.

Just off Burton Place behind the Police Station, stands an ominous-looking building with iron-barred windows and a hexagonal tower. This was Wilton Gaol, which opened in 1854 and was used up until 1884. There is a tunnel which runs to the Gaol from the Shire Hall, so the phrase "take him down" meant literally that.

Hangings took place at Wilton Gaol, apparently on the flat roof above its entrance and such events attracted eager spectators.

Let's just step back in time for a moment.

The year is 1854 or sometime after that. In Burton Place itself, just across the road from the prison, stands a row of small terrace houses. In the attic room of number 5, a woman is working as a seamstress or some very similar occupation. The floorboards are elm planks and shrinkage has left gaps between them.

Sometimes the Seamstress drops one of her ball-headed little copper pins and it falls through the gaps in the floorboards. Hanging from her blouse is a little 2-inch brass chain which has a half-inch brass safety pin at the top and a little silver coin hangs on the end of the chain. The pin becomes detached and the pin, chain and coin fall off and drop through a gap in the boards, just like the pins. She does not notice that she has lost it and carries busily on with her work.

The little coin on a chain may well have been made for her by her husband who was very probably a warder in the prison, because these were warders' cottages and it is a strange coincidence that the coin bears the same year as the opening date of the Gaol.

Warders Cottages on the right and Wilton Gaol on the top left in Burton Place. One day, well over a hundred years later, someone finds her pins and her coin on a chain. The finder was me. I still have that little chain and the coin is a silver fourpence, also known as a Groat, which was one-third of a shilling. The date on it is 1854.

I found the coin, together with some copper pins when I lifted the floorboards whilst I was rewiring the house for my brother Brian who had bought it as a place for his mother-in-law to live. At that time, he and his wife, Pauline, were living in and running St Georges Guest House just around the corner about 100 metres away.

Just a little way up the road on the near corner of Westgate Street is another little terrace house (number 21, it is the cream painted house in the above picture). It is easy to see that the prison, the warders' cottages and number 21 Westgate Street are all within yards of each other.

During their retirement years, Frederick John Adams and his wife Alice Maud lived in this house. They had been born in 1884 and 1883 respectively and they married in 1905. These people were my grandfather and grandmother.

In 1909, they were blessed with their second child and named him Albert Henry. This was my father.

Also in Westgate Street lived my auntie Dorothy (who we called auntie Dodo), her husband Reg, their adopted daughter Anne and my eldest brother Tony.

So this little area has obvious associations with my family and it is for that reason I chose this as the place to begin my story.

****

It was 1944 and events were moving towards the end of the Second World War. During May of that year, the BBC began broadcasting the first line of a well-known poem by the Frenchman Paul Verlaine.

"Les sanglots longues des violons de l'automne."

Which I believe means the long moaning sighs of the autumn winds.

This was a secret signal to the French Resistance and it meant INVASION WITHIN TWO WEEKS!

They knew this because they had British S.O.E. Agents among them who had been either parachuted in or landed in

Lysander planes, which could land at night in a small field. This remarkable little aircraft was built at Westlands of Yeovil, Somerset.

They used a little radio homing device called Rebecca/Eureka. The Rebecca unit was carried in the aircraft and the Eureka unit was on the ground. French Resistance members, standing in a remote field at night would have the Eureka device which received a directional signal from the aircraft and responded to it. The pilot of the Lysander obviously had the other device which received the response and homed-in on it. When the people on the ground heard the aircraft approaching, they would briefly point hooded flashlights towards the sound to guide it into a landing.

A quick drop-off or pick-up of an agent and it would take off into the darkness and was gone. The Germans knew what was happening. They would hear an aircraft somewhere and would rush around trying to find it but were unable to do so because it was gone and so were the Resistance people who had vanished into the darkness.

On the 4 June, the BBC broadcast the second line of the poem: "Blessent mon coeur d'une languor monotone."

Which I believe means: Wound my heart with their monotonous languor.

This meant INVASION WITHIN 24 HOURS!

This second line was the secret signal to units of the French Resistance instructing them to carry out pre-planned sabotage missions to help disrupt the German responses to the forthcoming invasion. They blew up railway lines and blasted down rows of telephone poles, for example.

Operation Overlord, the D-Day Normandy Landings took place on the 6 June 1944, with British Airborne Troops landing in Gliders shortly after midnight and quickly capturing the bridges over the Caen Canal and the River Orne.

A little later, American Paratroops descended from the skies in the area of St Mere Eglise, about 65 miles from the British landings.

At dawn, about 5000 ships appeared out of the sea mist and launched landing craft between the British and American Airborne Assaults on beaches codenamed:

Sword, Juno, Gold, Omaha and Utah.

I was born at No. 16 Wheatley Crescent, 11 weeks 3 days later on 30 August 1944, which makes me a Virgoan and, according to the Chinese calendar, a monkey!

On 8 September 1944, when I was just 8 days old, the Germans had finally got their V2 Rockets to work properly and they began what was intended to be a massive bombardment of London. This lasted until 27 March 1945, when the allies had advanced far enough to drive the launch sites back to take them beyond the range of London. Their intention had been to take Britain out of the war.

My name Kenneth is derived from the Celtic Caennech, meaning 'born of fire'. This would seem to fit me because I was obviously born during the war.

I now know, of course, that my mother named me Kenneth Roger. She had previously worked for Commander Kenneth Cary Helyar, who had a son named Roger.

Apparently, Commander Helyar had served in the First World War Naval battle of Zeebrugge. She named me after them both.

Commander Helyar is buried in the churchyard of his home village of Pitminster, about 3 miles from Taunton. His military-type headstone is near the footpath on the southern boundary. My father, grandfather, grandmother, sister Beryl, Uncle Reg and Auntie Dorothy (Dodo) and my dear wife Gillian, all lie in the same churchyard.

My mother always told me that she was the seventh child and that I was her seventh child.

A Mrs Sydenham (herself a medium), once told me the seventh of a seventh is always psychic.

I cannot claim to be able to contact or perceive spirits or any stuff like that, but I honestly believe I have an uncanny ability to 'see into' anyone's true self within seconds of eye contact and will 'know' whether they are good or bad-natured. I am a bit of a guitarist and it is my belief that anyone (like myself), who can actually be moved to tears by some music, has a 'real soul' and that not everyone possesses this.

I would not claim to be a good guitarist, but I find playing it very moving and therapeutic.

My father, Albert Henry Adams, was born at 19 Kingston Road, over a century ago on 23 March 1909 (died 18 August 1961 at Musgrove Park Hospital). His father, Frederick John Adams was born at Pitminster and his name appears on the little brass plaque in the village church doorway, under the heading 'Men of this village who served in the Great War'. He was, as mentioned, a Sapper in the Royal Engineers and he survived the Great War, although he was very badly shell-shocked for the rest of his life.

In the Entrance to Pitminster Church, the second inscription down is my grandad, ADAMS. F. J.

It has occurred to me that, as a boy, Dad would have seen the Trams that trundled up the Kingston Road hill past No. 19 (where he was born) and on to Gladstone Street Terminus, a little further on. This is very close to Taunton railway station.

On the road outside 19 Kingston Road. Photo courtesy of Nick Chipchase, Taunton Historian.

There was a turntable at the mouth of Gladstone Street just up the road from this picture, where the Trams were turned and returned down through the town to the other Terminus situated opposite Gray's Terrace at the other end of town. They operated on a single line, with passing loops at various locations along the way.

Dad grew up to become a bricklayer of the most unusual repute. At that time, bricklayers' mortar was known in the trade as 'Lappy'. It was from this that he got the nickname 'Lappy Adams'. He was so proficient at laying bricks at great speed that he needed two labourers to keep him supplied with mortar. One man could not keep up with him!

It is indeed unfortunate that at some time during his career, Dad became addicted to cider, the very strong drink made from apples for which Somerset is famous. Nowadays, alcoholism is recognised as an illness from which a person will probably never fully recover. I have heard from many sources that all the local builders knew about Dad and of his extraordinary ability to lay bricks at great speed. Some of them were unscrupulous enough to actually ply him with cider to get him to work for them.

I know that he was a wonderful craftsman at his work and that he would most likely have achieved much but for his addiction.

He was the foreman bricklayer on the project of building the hydrographic office for the Ministry of Defence (Navy), which was built to resemble the outline of a ship, Taunton was the chosen site because of its geographical location, midway between the great naval dockyards of Plymouth and Portsmouth.

It would seem appropriate that I include a photo for posterity in this book of an image I bought whilst employed there. The image shows Edgell Block and there were many other blocks named: Dalrymple, Beaufort, Walker, Franklin, Challenger, Bligh, Vidal and Dampier Blocks, spring to mind. They were all named after famous naval explorers, etc.

I am amazed that this building has now been demolished; it stood across the road from Asda supermarket car park and is now a flat site behind the Mercedes showrooms.

Picture from Hydrographic Office archives

Dad also worked on the rapid construction of the single-storey, Musgrove Park Hospital which consisted of many flat-roofed brick buildings, linked by open-sided covered walkways. It was, I believe, built with American money as a casualty receiving hospital in anticipation of the forthcoming Allied invasion of Normandy, operation 'overlord'.

Wartime Musgrove Hospital Entrance.

It would seem appropriate at this juncture, to mention an amusing little tale I heard about my father. At the age of about nineteen, he appears to have been something of a 'Laddo'.

He had apparently landed himself 'in hot water' with a woman I have chosen to describe as 'probably not of the highest repute'.

My grandfather was extremely worried about his son's forthcoming court appearance and expressed his fears to a farmer who lived near Pitminster Church and just along from the cottages where the woman concerned lived.

The Farmer said to my grandfather, "Oh—that place!"

He then said, "Don't worry, I will get him off."

Apparently, when summoned as a witness and questioned whether he had seen my father visiting the woman at her house, he replied, "Yes, I did see him visiting but I was not aware it was a house, I thought it was a recruiting office."

Apparently, the case was dismissed.

Our mother was always very fond of telling us of the days when she was in service as a scullery maid at Barton Grange, an imposing 'great house' at the time, standing in about 300 acres and which had lodge houses at each of the entrances from three villages, Pitminster, Corfe and Poundisford, just to the south of Taunton, in Somerset.

When Mum started work at Barton Grange at the age of about 12 years, I am told that she 'lived-in' in the servants' quarters for much of the time. When she received her monthly pay of about five shillings (about 50 pence today), she was allowed to go home for a few days and her stepmother, 'Auntie Kitt' as Mum knew her, would be waiting at the gatehouse to take all of her wages from her.

Sadly, all that now remains is the 'kitchen wing' of Barton Grange, which once had 365 windows.

From what Mum told us though, she did have some wonderful times during her four years at the Grange.

Barton Grange is today a mere shadow of its former grandeur, having been largely demolished in 1931. Only one wing is still standing and is used as a block of flats into which, it seems to have been converted by 'Gassy Harris', a well-known Taunton property owner. I am told that he sold the grand staircase and some Adam Fireplaces to someone in America. In its heyday, the Grange had 365 windows, the same as the number of days in a year.

I remember as a child, seeing a model of the Grange as it once was. The model was on display inside the entrance to Taunton Castle Museum, near a great steam-engine which had once worked at Messrs Pearsalls, Silk Throwsters in the town.

The 'Alice and Emma' have imposed on the engine beam photo were two of my ancestors who worked at Pearsalls.

Taunton Castle Museum, steam engine
Woolf compound beam engine of 1850 vintage by Easton & Amos of London. Used in Pearsall's silk mills in Taunton. Now preserved in the Taunton Castle Museum.

I have been told I have no proof of this, that the model of Barton Grange is the property of a family named Spurway and I believe that it had been on loan to the museum but has been returned to one of the Spurways who live at Corfe, just outside Taunton.

Mum always said that the gentleman she worked for and who lived there was Leonard Vaughan but I can find very few records of him.

Mum used to tell us how she travelled in style, when her employer, the owner of the Grange, would get his chauffeur to drive 'the girls' into Taunton in his Rolls Royce to the dances. Many of the dances would have been held at Claridges, London Hotel. It was called the Empire Ballroom, later the County Hotel and Ballroom. The site is now a Waterstones bookstore but is still marked 'The County'.

Then and now pictures of the Ballroom where Mum's employer had 'the girls' chauffeured to dances.

It is possible that Mum came to meet my father at one of these dances.

Mum got married after only about 4 years of working life at 'The Grange'.

Like so many others before and since it would appear that they 'had to' get married.

Mum had been born in the nearby village of Trull on 23 March 1907 and christened Dorothy Mary Hartnell.

I now know from my family research, that she lived with her parents there in a little terraced brick cottage at No 2. Southview Terrace, up the little lane, across the road from the side of the village church.

I did not discover this until years later. I used to visit my sister-in-law, Carol and her husband, Jeff, who by another strange coincidence, purchased this very same house as their first home when they married.

Mum's father was named William Hartnell, her mother, Emma Louisa (nee Smith).

Apparently, William was cheating on his wife (with her sister Kitt). People said that Emma died of a broken heart, she had lost two daughters, both of whom died of tuberculosis and William had made her sister Kitt pregnant. After the death of his wife, when my mother was nine years old, he married Kitt, who gave birth to a daughter and named her Evelyn. For some obscure reason, Evelyn became known as Dimp. I always knew her as Auntie Dimp.

Mum and Dad were married in 1925, Mum was about eighteen, Dad 16 or 17.

They lived at first, with my grandparents at Brookside Cottage, Pitminster, where they had their first child, Tony. They then moved to Winchester Cottage adjoining The Winchester Inn in the nearby village of Trull, where my sister Betty was born.

After moving to Elms Parade in Taunton, they got a council house at 16 Wheatley Crescent where I was the last born of this marriage on 30 August 1944.

In this, her first marriage, Mum had three daughters and four sons. Tony, Beryl, Betty, Brian, Jillarie, Colin and Ken (me).

The normal practice in those days was for a midwife from Canon Street Nursing Home to call and deliver a child at home. This was indeed the case when I arrived on the scene.

Apparently, my sister Betty became the 'little mother' when a child was born and she took care of the house and children in my mother's stead. The midwives were so impressed by one so young that they knitted a Fairisle Beret and gloves for her.

In later years, Betty always said she was the 'Cinderella' because her older sister (Beryl), did not join in with the chores.

Mum would have had to pay for the midwife to deliver me, as indeed for all her children because there was no NHS at that time.

Aneurin Bevan, the Great Statesman and Labour MP who founded the NHS.

The government took over responsibility for all medical services on 5 July 1948.

He resigned in 1951 when the government introduced charges for prescriptions and dental services.

We could certainly do with some politicians today who measure—up to his example!

****

Ours was obviously a large family, consisting of Mum and Dad and seven children.

There were eight people living in the three-bedroom house, so Mum's firstborn (Tony) who was diabetic and not expected to live to be older than about 14, needed care and so he had to go and live with our uncle Reg and auntie Dorothy. Auntie Dodo and Uncle Reg paid for his insulin treatments. They brought him up well and fortunately, he did not die that young. He actually lived to the age of 43 and was a dad to 4 children.

Dad's sister Dorothy, whom we called Auntie Dodo, lived in that already mentioned Westgate Street with her husband (Uncle Reg). They had no children of their own and I believe they were glad to have Tony with them. It may well also have been to give us more room in our overcrowded conditions. They also adopted a girl called Anne and brought her up.

Mum had to divorce Dad around 1947, she was left with 7 children to feed and bring up on her own. There were no benefits to be had so she needed to go to work.

So when Mum left Dad, through his drinking, she took her children (six of the seven) of us, with her, to Cutsey Farm, Trull for about three months. She was engaged there as a housekeeper. I have to say that I can't really ever remember much of Dad 'at home' so to speak. Being his 'youngest', I was approaching 3 years old when Mum finally 'chucked him out'. Then, they became divorced. I know that Dad had developed a very bad drinking problem.

I have vague memories of being at Cutsey Farm as a little boy. I can remember going up the stairs to bed with a candlestick because there was no electricity. I also remember the huge shire horses toying with me. I would be playing in the yard and they would nudge me with their heads.

Often, the farmer would sit me on the horse-drawn wagon and we would plod around the lanes to various farms. Each farm had a crude wooden platform by its entrance at the same height as our wagon and we would collect milk churns from them and leave empty ones. Sometimes, there were scattered ears of corn on the floor of the wagon and I would pick the corn out and chew it.

The local council made Dad vacate our house. He moved back in with his mum and dad at 21 Westgate Street. We all returned home to find our house virtually empty of furniture. Dad had sold it all. Mum went around all the second-hand shops, managed to locate it all and the shopkeepers agreed to let her buy it back at so much per week.

No Silver Spoon

He was born long after his siblings, most likely a mistake.

Couldn't have known his life would never be a piece of cake.

His father was a bricklayer, with a great degree of skill.

But he had the drink illness, which eventually would kill.

He was only two years old when his Mother left his dad.

Going to work as a housekeeper, the only choice she had.

Her work was at a local farm and she took all her brood.

The Farmer paid her meagrely but supplied them all with food.

Eventually, their dad moved out and then they moved back in.

But they very soon discovered he'd committed quite a sin.

He'd sold—off all their furniture and left the place quite bare.

They all had to sleep on the floor and make-do then and there.

Mum had to earn some money, there was no beneficial pool.

And to enable her to do so, the three-year-old went to school.

His footwear was from a jumble sale, two left shoes on his feet.

And after his infant school lessons, with his sister, he would meet.

His mum then met another man and very soon they wed.

The older siblings all left home, for him a stepbrother instead.

His stepfather was kind to his own son and pushed the boy aside.

He was always left at home when they went out for a ride.

At school, the boy was fairly bright and passed his 13-plus exam.

But was denied a place at Grammar School, by interview places scam.

Had to leave school when he was 15, earning money was the norm.

Instead of furthering his education, by staying in the sixth form.

His stepfather got him a job as an apprentice pattern-maker.

It seemed to him he didn't fit in and that he was the only taker.

The boy discovered he wanted to be an electrical engineer and left.

His boss became a despicable man and left him quite bereft.

Refused to give him a reference, gave him not one penny.

He tried to find a foothold, but there weren't very many.

And then he met a great man, an engineer who handed him a chance.

It was made very clear he'd have to work hard, without a song and dance.

The boy religiously went to college to try to better himself.

Whilst doing work that made his hands bleed, to get him off the shelf.

He went on to work for Western Power and British Telecom and he loved his new employ.

Then he worked for the M.O.D. and local government and I was that little boy!

By: The Author: 22 August 2020.

****

We lived in absolute poverty and this was in the time of war rationing, which restricted us still further. We had tins of 'National' milk powder, egg powder, cod liver oil and radio malt which were issued by the government to supplement the diet of the population.

Mum then got a job as a canteen lady at the local company called Clement & Brown and as a consequence of that, I had to go to St James School at the age of just three years. My brother and sister took me to St. James School and collected me every day. We would then walk home and wait for Mum to come home from work.

Although I obviously cannot recall everything, I do quite vividly remember a few little things that happened, like losing my silver ring down a drain at the corner of the school. The ring had been made for me by a German prisoner from a silver threepence. The teachers would not listen to my pleadings. I often wonder if someone found it or indeed if it is even still there!

St James School, which I had to go to at age 3 and the drain down which I lost my silver ring made by a German prisoner-of-war.

I also remember that we each had a little coconut mat each, on which we were supposed to go to sleep in the afternoons after drinking our free school milk. They were special little bottles of one-third of a pint, which were, I believe, specially bottled for schoolchildren. I cannot complain, though in any way about having to go to school so young. I was actually given a wonderful start in life when, at that tender age, I was taught to read by Miss Santler. She was a little old lady teacher at that time and I often wonder what became of her. The last I remember of her was when she was taken to hospital after a cord-operated window she was opening fell out of its casement onto her.

When I subsequently attended Priory Junior School, I, of course, could already read quite fluently. The teacher would get me to stand at the front of the class and read aloud to the class from our little 'Dick and Dora' books.

Priory Junior School, which I attended at age 5 after leaving St James School, which I went to at age 3.

Every single bit of clothes I wore was either 'hand-me-downs' or bought from a jumble sale.

Something else, though, is not so wonderful and amusing. My mum used to attend 'jumble sales' to get items of clothing and shoes very cheaply for us—simply because we were so poor. She had once bought a pair of shoes for me, which turned out to be 'not actually a pair'. She had inadvertently picked up two left shoes and bought them in the scramble. It would seem that someone must have bought two right shoes!

I had to wear the two 'left' shoes and they hurt one of my feet a lot. I had no choice, it was the only pair of shoes I had!

I distinctly remember my painful feet caused by wearing two left shoes and they were too small and very tight. I still have malformed feet to this day.

We all had to wear 'hand-me-down clothes' from the older children of our family.

If any of the boys complained about 'too big' trousers or something like that, Mum would say, "If you don't wear them, I'll put knickers and a skirt on you and send you to school like that."

When I see how fussy and spoilt children are today, refusing to wear anything which isn't 'cool', 'designer' and very expensive as well, I can only think they don't realise how lucky they are.

In the top right of this aerial photograph, is Hamilton Park and the road running along its side is Hamilton Road. The building on the triangle was a Telephone Repeater Station and is now a church. The road alongside it which runs up to the house where I was born is Wheatley Crescent. Where the road went around to the left, is now a turning left as it now actually goes straight on and runs down past Asda on the left and the UK Hydrographic on the right. The filled-in gully was the dumping ground for all the demolished air-raid buildings in

Taunton. 'Our house' is now gone and replaced by a modern development.

Our council house, like all those in the area, was built of solid, cast concrete which had been pebble-dashed to give a presentable appearance. It had an uninsulated slate roof and was very cold in the winter as there were no cavity walls.

The ground-floor consisted of a little entrance porch, a 'front room' as we called it and a 'scullery' as Mum called it. The front room had windows looking out on both the front and back gardens. It contained a fireplace, a sofa and a few chairs, a sideboard, a lino on the floor and a 'wind up' gramophone, which stood on four legs and had a winding handle on the side.

On lifting the lid, the deck would be revealed and there was a shiny tubular metal 'pick-up' which had to be lowered onto the record by hand. There was also a little tray, which contained metal needles for the pick-up and if they weren't sharp would give a fuzzy reproduction through the little 'sound box', which was mounted on the pick-up arm. It played big '78 RPM' records and as the clockwork mechanism 'ran down' the music and voice would go slow and deep sounding, which we thought was hilarious.

The front room was painted with white distemper, which was a powder mixed in a bucket with water. I can remember helping to improve the appearance, as we did in those days. We would each have a little ball of cotton wool, which we would dip into saucers of coloured distemper and make fuzzy blobs of colour with them all over the walls. We did this because we were poor. Nowadays, I see programs such as 'changing rooms' and '60-minute make-over' on television in which they regard similar ideas as 'cool'.

I can also remember Mum grabbing me as a small child and hiding us together behind the sofa when she heard the Rent Man knocking at the door. On one occasion, the Rent Man went around the back of the house and looked through the other window. He saw us hiding from his view through the front window. Mum must have felt a complete fool when she went to the door and made her excuses.

The scullery had a brick floor which Mum used to scrub on her hands and knees using a hard green block of 'Puritan' soap, a coarse bristled scrubbing brush with a wooden back shaped like an hourglass and a cloth with which she would mop up the excess water and then wring it out into a bucket.

Mum always used to say, "It doesn't matter how poor you are, there's no excuse for filth."

There was a Belfast-type sink on brick pillars, a cold water tap and a grooved wooden draining board, which also had to be scrubbed.

There were no refrigerators in those days, the larder had a thick stone slab as one of its shelves and behind that shelf was a small window which had a sheet of perforated zinc instead of glass.

Our means of cooking and heating was what we called 'The Range'. This was made of cast iron and built into the chimney breast. The fire basket burnt coal or logs and beside it was the oven, which was heated by the fire. Kettles or pans would be placed over the fire, as would a solid 'flat iron' with which Mum did her ironing.

We had to have coal and any old wood we could lay our hands on.

It was very rare indeed for Mum to afford a bag of coal, so Mum would send us with a pram or one of our homemade trolleys to either Starr's Garage which had a coal yard or to the other coal yard behind Gregory's Grocer shop on Hamilton Road near the Rose Inn. Mum would tell us to ask the coal yard man for sixpence worth of 'Nutty Slack'. Using this as fuel was advised by the government because of shortages.

It was 'dirty burning' stuff and is thought to have caused the smog.

He would then shovel us up some coal dust and fragments from the coal piles into his open-fronted weighing scuttle and tip it into our sack. I am absolutely sure he felt sorry for us little poor kids because he would throw a few lumps of coal into our sack when no one was looking and give us a wink.

Starr's Garage and Coal Yard.

The house in the background is No. 1 Gray's Terrace and my eldest brother Tony owned it for a while and lived there with his wife and family.

Our 'bathroom' was a galvanised steel bath about one metre long, hanging on a nail in the scullery.

This would be placed on the brick floor one night a week and filled with water from kettles and pans heated on the range. The rule was eldest first and so on but we all bathed in the same water, albeit with an occasional top-up because it was losing its heat.

We all had to take turns to bathe in the same water, in a galvanised bath which was normally kept hung on the wall in the shed. We would bring it into the scullery, place it on the brick floor and Mum would heat kettles and pans of water on the range.

Sitting in the bath in the scullery, all we had was a big green block of 'Puritan' soap, which was also used for washing clothes and for scrubbing the brick floor. The Range was a black iron thing, which was made to burn coal and heat the iron oven which was part of it. Kettles, etc., had to be put over the fire and we burnt anything we could get our hands on, mainly bits of scrounged wood we could cut up. We only had a very blunt old saw and would rub a candle or soap on it to stop it from jamming in the wood or logs we were cutting up.

Mum also had a smaller galvanised bath into which she put hot water from the range. With the very same block of soap and a little blue block about the size of an Oxo Cube for whitening and her 'poking stick', she did our laundry. This was her 'washing machine'. We had a big cast iron mangle with wooden rollers and I would turn the handle as she fed the washing into it. It would squeeze the items of clothing between the rollers and all the squeezed-out water returned to the bath which was placed under the mangle via a little chute.

We were always hungry and had to eat everything we were given, which was not much.

We had a long-handled fork which was made out of twisted wire. We would put a bit of bread on the fork and hold it close to the fire in the range to toast it. Once toasted, we would spread dripping on it and then eat it. Even the stale bread was toasted and eaten.

There was no television, we would sit around the range listening to the radio and we had a long fork made from a twisted wire on which we would impale a piece of bread and toast it on the flames of the range. This would be spread with 'dripping' (the white fat residue collected from cooking meat). The brown gritty bits around the edges of the fat in the bowl were delicious!

One of the radio programmes I remember was entitled *Journey into Space* and I would sit wide-eyed and fascinated whilst listening.

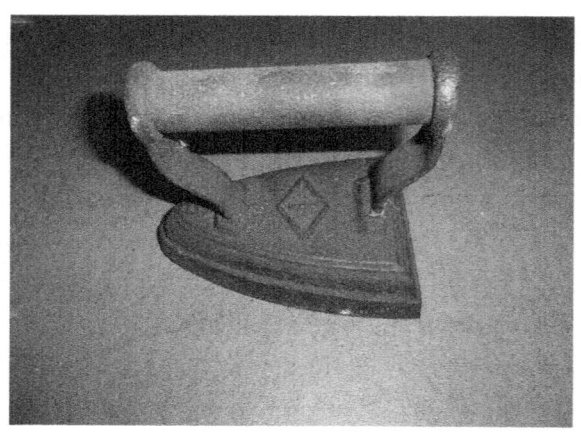

A flat iron, just like Mum had to use!

So there were many things which are now so taken for granted. We had no washing machine, no spin dryer, no fridge, no cooker, no television, no car and not even such a simple thing as an electric iron or kettle. Everyone then used a flat iron which had to be heated on the range.

The roads were almost devoid of cars by comparison to now and there was a little old lady who used to come around the streets sitting on a plodding horse-drawn wagon loaded with vegetables. She would be constantly shouting out how much her potatoes were per pound, etc. and people would come out and buy from her. There was often a free 'bonus' to be had. People would rush out with a bucket to collect the horse's droppings. They would use it in the garden for their rhubarb!

One vehicle we would often see, though, was a little articulated GWR truck with a single front wheel. We had a Goods Station like most towns and these little trucks delivered to all the shops and so on. Much of what is carried all over the country by thousands of trucks nowadays was carried by the goods trains. What a step backwards that was! One goods train could carry the equivalent of about thirty modern trucks over distance and what huge amounts of pollution is caused now by all those trucks?

I do remember well though, that each Friday night my sister Jill and my brother Colin would take me with them to visit Dad and we would all walk from one side of Taunton to the other. That is from Wheatley Crescent to 21 Westgate Street, where my dad had gone back to live with his mum and dad. Being the baby, my dad would sit me on his knee and make a fuss over me. I feel sure he loved his children and it is very sad that he had succumbed to the demon drink.

I know now that we were basically sent there by Mum to get money from Dad for our 'keep'.

Dad would always make quite a fuss of me and was very proud of his work, he would show me blueprints of projects he had built or was building. He was actually the foreman bricklayer during the building of the hydrographic office.

Also, in Hamilton Road were the post office and Mr C. Webber's cycle shop next door. We could buy ball bearings, chain links and anything for a bike there when we were trying to make a bike from bits obtained from the local tip. Mr Webber was well-known in the town because he used to ride a penny-farthing bicycle in the annual carnival procession.

Other shops were Sully's Grocery shop on Roman Road, where we had to take our post-war ration books to get things. There was a tiny little cobbler's shop in the same street owned by Mr Toller, it was so small that only one person could enter and stand at his little counter at a time.

The tiny shop stood on the southwest corner of what is today's Lidl Car Park. We boys used to get Mr Toller to put metal studs in the heels of our shoes which made an impressive loud clicking sound as we walked on them and were supposed to save the heels from wear. We would kick our heels along the ground and make sparks fly from them.

Shades of the 1940s

When I was just a little boy, we didn't have a lot. My mother kept the lights on, with a shilling in the slot.

No TV, just a radio, that too was on the meter, but when I cast my mind back, life then was so much sweeter.

The larder wasn't always full of tasty things to eat, but we didn't notice hunger as we played out in the street.

Our clothes weren't always bought new, quite often worn before. We didn't follow fashion, never thought to ask for more.

My mother's purse was empty, except of course for dreams but she always found some pennies to buy us some ice cream.

Our shoes were always from a jumble sale. Our hair was never neat, very difficult indeed to take care of your feet.

Free school milk was granted, given by the state. We looked as smart as anyone when we walked through that school gate.

In summer, we picked blackberries from the hedgerows in the field, our fingers stained with purple as we delighted in our yield.

No game consoles to keep us quiet, our joy was climbing trees, grass stains on our knees, from where we used to play.

We didn't have a single care, as night just followed day.

The girls would make their perfume with petals from the flowers, often getting in hot water 'cos the blooms were never ours.

We shared bikes and shared footballs, used our jumpers as the goal and when the bitter weather came, filled buckets up with coal.

Every single chimney cast plumes into the sky as we huddled by the fire with a pasty or a pie.

Scratch your name on the frosty pane before the curtains close, tucked under a heap of blankets—no choice but to stay put.

We never had a holiday. Certainly not abroad, a day in sunny Weston was all we could afford.

We'd paddle in the Bristol Channel and sit down in the foam, ride a donkey up the beach and wish we could take it home.

Our kitchen was always full of steam from laundry and the mangle, there was no electric washing machine to get it in a tangle.

We made toast on the open fire I can taste it to this day, dripping in salted butter it seems half a world away.

Every Christmas there were presents under our tinselled tree and always we were overjoyed whatever they may be In and out of houses up and down the street, borrowing cups of sugar helped to make ends meet.

We didn't have a telephone so we couldn't run up a bill. We only tasted Lucozade when we were gravely ill.

The doctor saw you on the sofa with his stethoscope and bag. A week off school was endless if you succeeded with the blag.

Life back then was infinite you never could grow old, there was nothing to be frightened of with your mother's hand to hold.

Death was never mentioned, too young to understand, it seemed that life would just work out the way you had it planned.

But the time passed in minutes there was no time to spare, overnight it seemed the silver threads adorned your mother's hair.

Your endless days were over as time raced away at pace and the happy days of innocence disappeared without a trace.

Don't waste a single minute of this life with which you're blessed, things change in just a heartbeat the ride can come to rest.

Good times become just memories, faces fade and smiles are lost, don't wish away a second hang on at any cost.

When I was just a little boy, we didn't have a lot, but one day all that nothing, will be the greatest gift I've got!

'When I was just a little Girl', By Sarah Morris Armer

Brother Colin, sister Jillarie and me in the centre, at our house in Wheatley Crescent.

I think that Mum and Dad must have had one of the three bedrooms to themselves and that we three boys Brian, Colin and myself had one of the other rooms, whilst our sisters, Beryl, Betty and Jillarie must have shared the remaining one.

I can vaguely remember sleeping in a double bed between my 'big brothers' and was often very uncomfortable or too hot. I am sure I experienced recurring nightmares because of such sleeping arrangements. My sister knows that I told her I had seen 'a man walk through the wall'. I still don't know whether it was a nightmare or I had seen a ghost!

My sisters would go to local shops and scrounge empty orange boxes to make bedside cabinets. They would stand them on end and cover them with wallpaper.

A bit of flexible curtain wire was stretched across the front top edge to hold a curtain, which gave the finishing touch.

The electricity meter was a 'coin in the slot' type and it took a one shilling coin only.

Often, Mum wouldn't have that much so we had to cut a halfpenny coin by furiously chiselling about 5mm off of it with the aid of a hammer whilst resting the coin on a bit of wood. The coin would then fit into the meter and give us another shilling worth of electricity.

When the man came around to empty the meter about once a month, he would count the shillings and deduct one shilling from 'the rebate' for every cut halfpenny. He would then hand the cut halfpennies back to us. The rebate was always eagerly anticipated because it represented a sort of 'savings' and was very welcome to families so desperately short of money.

At the front of our house was a small garden with a low concrete boundary wall with a single strand of wire strung between posts to add height. I can still remember, as a very small boy, clambering about on the low wall whilst holding onto the strand of wire. One day I had a twisted end of the wire caught under my silver threepence ring and it took me ages to free myself. I couldn't get down off the wall until I had done so.

Me on my 'MOBO' bike in our back garden. The youngest photo I possess.

I also remember playing one of my favourite games. I would roll myself up on an old rug on the lawn and pretend I was in a spaceship and going to the moon.

I remember learning to ride a bike whilst we were living at Wheatley Crescent. I obviously fell off a few times and suffered knee grazes and the like, but was undeterred and soon found myself pedalling around the square with great excitement.

So excited was I, that when Johny Adams (not related to me), tried to get his bike back from me, I punched him and made his nose bleed. His dad came out and clipped my ear and took it from me. I went running indoors with a singing ear shouting, "Mum, I can ride a bike!"

****

Our back garden was long and narrow and ended in a rough hedge at its eastern end. Beyond the hedge, was what had been a long deep overgrown gully, which ran parallel to a footpath which we called Roman Lane and which incidentally is still there. It was about 20 metres wide from our hedge to the footpath and it sloped upwards from Roman Road at its southerly end to its summit behind our house and then downhill past the end of Moorland Road to its end near Valley Road.

I personally do not remember it as a gully, as my earliest years were just after the Second World War and the gully had been partially filled in with all the materials from the demolished air-raid shelters from around Taunton.

From the Valley Road end, a rough lane ran behind the houses of Beadon Road and then emerged at a little brick culvert over a small stream very close to the perimeter fence of the Hydrographic office. Today, during 2017, the entrance to the hydro is right where the little culvert was alongside the fairly new Mercedes Showroom.

I remember the gully as an overgrown area of rough ground which had great slabs of still joined brickwork and thick slabs of concrete protruding from the ground in which it lay half-buried, at all angles.

At the bottom of our garden, which was always planted with various vegetables for the kitchen, was a rough hedge on an earthen bank. Naturally, we had a quick way through into the waste ground beyond.

I remember the rough ground interspersed with great jutting angular blocks of thick brickwork and concrete. It was a rough area about 10 metres wide and it ran downhill to the right for about 100 metres parallel to the hedge until it reached Roman Road. I am told that the gully had been filled with all the remains of the demolished air-raid shelters from around the town.

This must have been done not long after I was born. It was a paradise for us kids to play in, there were bramble bushes from which we could pick blackberries in season and we would use the longer sections of angled brickwork as playground slides, clambering up the rough edges and sliding down the shiny brick faces on the seat of our pants!

On the far side of the gully was a footpath, elevated in places, which we called Roman Lane. We would sit on a piece of wood with a roller skate underneath and roll precariously down the footpath, steering by leaning to the left or right.

The predecessor of today's skate boards! There was a strong possibility of skinning your knuckles if you leaned a bit too much, though. If we were lucky enough to find an old pram thrown out, we would make what we called a trolley by fixing one pair of wheels under a plank and the other pair to a narrow piece of wood which had a bolt through it and the other end of the plank. The bolt formed the front steering. The axles were fixed to the wood by nails driven half in and then bent over the axle.

Various crude braking devices were tried, but none of them worked, so spills were commonplace and so were bruises and grazes!

The footpath and the gully also ran downhill to the left until it reached the dead end of Moorland Road, where the footpath ended and the gully continued down to Valley Road and then on over a brick culvert and along the fence of 'The Admiralty' as we called the hydrographic office.

I am told that sometimes Dad would have a small barrel of cider in our brick shed in the garden. There was at least one occasion when my older brothers sampled it and got quite drunk. They were found fast asleep from the effects!

In our back garden, we had a few chickens in a 'chicken run' as did many people in those days. The cage was basically a wire-mesh affair fixed to any old bits of wood and a wooden hen house attached at one end with nesting boxes for the hens.

It was a general practice to keep chickens in those days.

We would go to Taunton Market and start helping farmers get their sheep into pens.

Sometimes the farmer would give us sixpence as a tip. If we got enough money, we would buy a couple of little yellow chicks from the covered market, would take them home and rear them in an orange box with a light bulb to keep them warm. When they had grown into egg-laying pullets, they provided a valuable supplement to our food, especially during the rationing years which followed the war.

Once they were ready to start laying eggs, we would put them in our wire mesh chicken run with laying boxes. That was how we got our eggs and once they stopped laying, the hen was for the cooking pot.

The chickens were fed on all the scrapings from dinner plates, etc. and all the potato peelings were saved in a bucket of water. The peelings would be boiled and fed to the chickens, along with perhaps a handful of bran.

I used to love going to collect the eggs from the laying boxes, they were often still warm in my hand.

The only trouble was, we had a cock bird. We called him Dickie Drumstick!

He would peck your legs quite viciously if you let him. It was a good insurance to take a little stick with you with which to hold him at bay. His Lordship was obviously very jealous of his hens.

When a chicken stopped laying eggs, it would be destined for the table. It would be held upside down by the legs and killed by a blow to the head with a length of wood.

I distinctly remember watching my big brother, Brian, knock a chicken on the head with a piece of wood to kill it. He then hung it on the clothesline by its feet and stuck a penknife back down its throat to 'bleed' it, followed by plucking out the feathers.

I, as a small boy, was obviously fascinated at watching the whole gory process and said, "Now do Kitty." I don't think our cat would have been very impressed by my suggestion!

Whilst on the subject, I also remember another amusing incident involving a chicken.

Our neighbour at No. 15, was a man called Edgar Voysey, Edgar was a milkman and lived with his sister whom he called Win. I remember her with her hair in a headscarf tied with a bow at the front and a perpetual fag in her mouth. Her appearance was that of a stereotypical charwoman.

One day, Edgar came rushing into our scullery and was ashen-faced. He said, "Oh my God, you've got to help me, Mrs Adams, there's a chicken running around in my kitchen."

Someone went in to investigate and found a naked chicken running about. Apparently, Edgar had 'killed and plucked' it, the only problem was that he hadn't got the 'killed' bit quite right!

I was told by my sister Betty that Edgar was somewhat naïve. He had, apparently, come running to our house, hammered on the door and told my mother, "Win's got a terrible stomach-ache."

She was, of course, pregnant and in labour. Mum tore up some old sheets and went next door! She told Eric to boil some water, to which he replied, "I'm not making any tea."

It was 'uncertain' what Win did for a living, but she had a son out of wedlock, Johny Voysey, who was a playmate of mine.

We also had rabbits on the menu, which were caught using ferrets. The procedure was to peg nets over the rabbit holes and then introduce a ferret. The ferret would drive the rabbits out and into the nets, from which we would extract them and dispatch them with a 'rabbit punch' behind the head. We would 'paunch' them on the spot because it's easier whilst they are still warm.

One of the rabbit's hind legs was then tucked under one's belt and the other leg threaded through it between the leg bones after the insertion of a penknife. That was the easy way to carry them. It all seems very cruel now, but it was done for food during post-war rationing of meat and we also used to take them around to our neighbours who would be very happy to buy them for threepence each. In today's money, this amounts to about 1.25 p, yes, one and a quarter pence!

You would be hard-pressed to buy a joint of meat at that price nowadays!

When we went rabbiting, we would be accompanied by our dog Toby, who was a very fit and active mongrel. The numerous rabbit holes would be covered with nets and then a ferret introduced into the warren. The ferret would panic the occupants into rushing out into the nets. Toby would catch any that escaped the nets.

One of Toby's amusing practices was jumping onto the rear platform of the local bus and going into town sitting there to look for Mum. Upon spotting her in the shopping crowds, he would jump off the platform of the moving bus and accompany her with a wildly wagging tail.

I can remember being made a great fuss of by two German prisoners-of-war.

They were, I believe, working as Labourers at a Military Establishment at Norton Fitzwarren just outside Taunton. I think it was called Army 3rd SRD (meaning Supply Reserve Depot). For many years after the war, these buildings still stood, they were enormous red brick warehouses with corrugated roofs. They were on the left as you drove up the hill from the Cross Keys Pub towards Norton Fitzwarren.

I believe the military was concerned about the risk of it being bombed and very probably the same risk to Taunton's vital hydrographic office (admiralty charts).

Again from my research, I have discovered that they built 2 Decoy sites which could burn oil and tar to make German Bombers think they had found target markers or already bombed targets. The code name for such sites was 'Starfish'. There was one at Castlemans Hill, Duddlestone just to the south of Taunton and one in the fields on the left at the top of Nynehead Hollow between Taunton and Wellington.

In later years, I remember my mum saying, "The Poles set fire to the hills and the Germans bombed the fires, the next day Lord Haw Haw boasted that Taunton had been bombed." He was an Irish/American propagandist named William Joyce, working for the Germans. He would begin his radio broadcasts by saying "Germany calling—Germany calling" and would speak with an upper-class English accent. People would listen to him and curse him as a traitor. He was wrong, of course, because they had aimed their bombs at the Starfish Decoys.

My father brought the German prisoners to our home. I now know that their names were Fritz Wock and Werner Tonedorf who were probably captured in Normandy. It was one of these men who made a ring for me from a silver—threepence. I was told by my older sisters that even after they were moved some twelve miles away, they would still often walk that distance to visit us, picking wildflowers along the way for my mother whom they called 'mutter', which is apparently German for 'mother'.

I can also remember that my brother Brian, who was obviously fond of me, would sit beside me and fondle my ears.

Opposite today's ASDA is a hill which I refer to in this book. It is known as Creech Barrow Hill, but all the local kids used to call it Captain Beadon's Hill. Right under the hill is Beadon Road.

Only fairly recently did I learn that the Captain Beadon referred to, appears to have been George Beadon, born at Gotton House near Taunton in 1810.

He joined the Royal Navy on 20 August 1825 (so he was only 15) and he appears to have risen to the rank of commander in 1841. He invented and patented an 'Improved Life-Buoy' for Seamen escaping from stricken ships.

The word 'Barrow' implies that the hill was manmade but it is actually a natural feature.

The hill is one of several similar ones dotted around the Somerset landscape, such as Burrow Mump, Brent Knoll and the world-famous Glastonbury Tor with the St Michael tower on its summit. The 'Holy Thorn' and Chalice Well are nearby.

Arthurian legend has it that this area was Avalon, the 'isle of glass', which was supposed to have been a huge expanse of shallow water, dotted with islands.

This would appear to make sense, given the natural hills mentioned sticking up out of the Somerset levels, (which are still prone to flooding even today).

Incidentally, I once read a book about Ley Lines and apparently, there is one called the St Michael Line. I don't honestly know whether such things exist or what they might actually be but have noticed on a map, that the St Michael Tower atop the world-famous Glastonbury Tor seems to be on a straight line which passes from there through Burrow Mump St Michael Tower, West Lyng St Michael Tower and on through Creech St Michael. That does seem to be a bit more than a coincidence, especially when you consider that many churches were built on previously pagan sites.

In my childhood, there was a green wedge, with its point reaching almost into the centre of the town, but anyone driving into Taunton nowadays from the M5 motorway along Toneway or approaching by train from the east, will see Creechbarrow Hill on the left-hand side. From the road, they would also see a military-type road sign, which announces that the United Kingdom Hydrographic Office (M.O.D.) is to the left and actually nestles under the hill.

This, though, may soon change because they have just built (2019) a new single building which will accommodate their whole operation.

I understand that all the old blocks are soon to be demolished and the land sold off for development.

This will probably mean that their new entrance will be either within the development or from Bridgwater Road near their 'Little Mariners' creche.

The original building has a somewhat sinister appearance, the brickwork still bore traces of camouflage paint, which was intended to break up its outline from prying eyes from the air during the Second World War and until recently, there was still an old Nissen hut, with its corrugated iron roof near the northern boundary fence.

Now, a Mercedes Showroom stands where it once stood. There was always a rumour that there were secret underground tunnels from the hydrographic office under Creechbarrow Hill. The original building was a camouflage-painted one which resembled the outline of a ship.

I actually worked there as plant engineer electrical from 3 July 1995 until 30 April 2004 (when I walked out never to return) after my long dispute with one of my bullying managers whom I considered to be incompetent and who covered his tracks by bluff.

During my time there, I had reason to access the tunnel that actually ran under the machine room where it carried various services under the huge printing machines. I feel sure someone before me had seen the entrance to that tunnel and had suspected that it ran under the hill. Hence the rumour!

Today, the entrance to the 'Admiralty' as we used to call it (the hydrographic office), is situated behind the Mercedes showrooms which were built in 2004 (opposite Asda), but there was only high-security fencing at this spot during my childhood. The entrance at that time, was about 100 metres around the perimeter to the south at the bottom of a street called crossways.

Creechbarrow Hill is fenced off now to become part of the Hydrographic but once formed part of the area I played in as a child. There was no motorway and the route into Taunton was via the infamous A38 which ran further to the south than the new road, along Hamilton Road and must have been cursed by motorists a thousand times when the holiday traffic used to jam it.

The new (Toneway) road is actually built over part of the former route of the River Tone. At this point, the road, river, railway and canal all run parallel to each other. The river formerly meandered along here, running from west to east.

The river from the town bridge, actually ran over the Firepool Weir to a lower level and on along roughly its present route, parallel to the Taunton-Bridgwater Canal.

There was a wooden bridge from Priory Fields across the river to the Canal Towpath, about 150 metres east of Firepool Weir and a man had a little business there on a bit of wasteland between the canal and the river and immediately east of the bridge. He was buying old railway sleepers, cutting them up and chopping them into firewood, which he tightly bundled with twisted wire. He sold them to the shops.

The river also ran across behind the weir so it went in two directions.

This part of the river continued from behind the weir (at the higher level) and it ran eastwards along behind the rugby ground (which has been built on and is now Geoffrey Farrant Walk and Wintersfield). It then curved south-eastwards and then eastwards to run roughly parallel to Priory Avenue to the locks, mill stream, a footbridge and an island which was at the lower level after passing over the lock-gates at the island and the end of the millstream.

The river then turned north and went on to rejoin the northern section of the river which ran from the bottom of Firepool Weir to become a single riverbed again, running out towards Bathpool. The point where it rejoined the northern section from Firepool, was just across a small field from the Obridge Canal bridge which is still there, not far from the point where people emerge from the modern Toneway underpass.

There was a big black pipe about 2 feet in diameter running on brick piers about 10 feet above the ground, running parallel to the footpath across this field. It was a sewage pipe and it crossed the river over its own girder bridge, running from west to east into the sewage treatment works on the east side of the river. This bridge was only about 20 metres from the bridge running north which you crossed on your way towards Obridge from the locks and the island, which led into the fields.

The river was extensively widened, deepened and straightened out some years ago in a flood prevention exercise, which worked. 'The Island' is now under the east car park of the present-day 'Wickes DIY' warehouse and the actual river coming from Firepool to the west of the island, ran north under where the warehouse itself now stands.

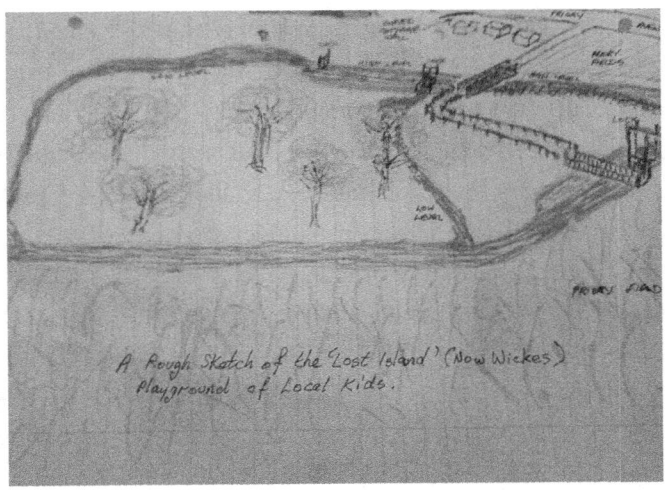

A Rough Sketch of the 'Lost Island' (Now Wickes) Playground of Local Kids.

Obridge Viaduct is a modern new road with a bridge which now spans the river, the railway and the canal. the southern leg of the river ran roughly parallel to Priory Avenue, across what is now the car park for all the warehouses and 'The (now lost) Island' as we kids called it was located from the left of the edge of the roundabout to the corner of the Wickes Warehouse, under the two trees.

The row of warehouses and their car park to the left is still called Priory Fields (which it once was) and the one nearest the roundabout is now 'Wickes Superstore'. The other trees are virtually running along the now buried riverbed, because Priory Avenue was diverted north into the fields, from where it originally went straight into what is now Monks Close.

The solitary house immediately above the words 'Monks Close' is the one with the old curved wall I remember so well. The modern house replaced an old cottage which stood there at the time but the wall is original. Still above the words 'Monks Close' and just to the right of the house is a tiny building. This is the little electricity substation shown in the other photos, with the original end of Wheatley Crescent sign showing.

'The Island' was one of the favourite venues for us kids. The whole area is much changed now because the river was diverted and filled in.

At the other end of the filled-in section, near the (now demolished) Cattle-Market in Canal Road, are the lock-gates which connected the Grand Western (Tiverton to Taunton) and the Bridgwater and Taunton Canals via the River Tone and nearby are the weir called Firepool. The water still tumbles over the weir and follows the new route of the river. The other end of the 'navigable' part of the river is at French

Weir Avenue. Over a little parapet is an overgrown gully which was the continuation of the canal where it then ran parallel to the river into Roughmoor.

There is a little electricity substation still standing at the end of Wheatley Crescent at the junction with what was Priory Avenue which is now the little renamed section of houses called Monks Close. This little section had been part of Priory Avenue, but you can clearly see how it was turned into a short Cul-de-sac when Chritchard Way, the busy roundabout and Toneway were built and chopped those houses off from the rest of Priory Avenue.

The 'chopped-off' section of Priory Avenue, which was renamed as Monks Close at the end of Wheatley Crescent, the old curved wall I refer to, is still there. Behind the trees is Chritchard Way, which chopped-off Priory Avenue when it was built.

You can just see a yellow part of today's Wickes Superstore (to the right of the house) which now stands in the old Priory Fields on the site of 'The Island' which was in the river. The car is facing down the road that leads to the old mill.

Emerging from Wheatley Crescent by the Substation as we kids did, just across the road, one of the houses of Monks Close was Mr Dare's shop up the steps. Back on the substation side of the road at the entrance to Monks Close is a curved stone wall with a modern house behind it. That stone wall has been there since I was a child but there was a thatched cottage behind it.

We used to walk past the cottage and were, of course, in Priory Avenue as it then was. Immediately after the cottage was a little cluster of about 2 semi-detached houses and then there was a narrow cinder footpath running north, with Priory Fields to the left of the footpath and the last house on the right.

This was the point where we used to enter Priory Fields. The cinder track ran over a lattice pattern iron girder bridge, which crossed a mill stream running towards the right and this wall formed the southern edge of 'The Island' as we kids called it.

The millstream had a brick and concrete retaining wall about 6 feet wide, which you could walk on. When I was about 8 years old, I was not there but one of my friends named Colin Sutton drowned in the millstream. The mill once stood roughly where the Deane DLO Council Workshops now stand. (Deane DLO is now being demolished in 2017).

Over the bridge, turning sharply to the left there was a short continuation of the cinder lane from which one could gain access to another footbridge over the lower water side of the lock-gates which were on the left as one crossed the footbridge. The other side of the bridge opened out into Priory Fields. You could either walk across the gradually narrowing fields between the high side of the river on your left and the low side of it on your right till you reached Firepool or you could turn right after crossing the bridge and walk alongside the river towards Obridge and Bathpool.

Because of the lock you had crossed, you were now following the lower level of the river. The island was on your right and you were approaching the point where the two separate river beds would merge to become one again.

'The Island' as we called it was a wonderful play area for us; there were trees, bushes, brambles and reeds growing on it. We would build a camp from branches and reeds and make bows and arrows, have a campfire and play there for hours.

Now, it is gone, buried and built over—so this is one of my 'Lost Islands'.

****

Lambrook Road in those days ran from the old GPO Repeater Station (now Riverside Church) opposite Hamilton Park along past the junction with Leycroft Road and then ran into Priory Avenue (at the beginning of what is now Monks Close).

Mr Jarman's fish and chip shop was on Leycroft Road to the left of the lane leading into Victoria Park. Mr Jarman was a quite chubby man and he had a deep groove on his forehead which we always thought had been caused by shrapnel, he was a kind-hearted man and would come out to us kids playing in front of his shop and say, "Want some scrumps kids?"

He knew we had no money. We would eagerly all say, "Yes please, Mr Jarman," Then he would give each of us a little chip bag full of fried batter pieces which had fallen off the fish.

On the other side of the lane was the Co-op dairy and I remember watching many times in fascination, the milk bottle washing machines and the loudly clattering machines which filled the bottles and put foil caps on them of different colours which denoted the various types of milk. There were also milk bottles in those days with a cardboard disc for a top.

This cardboard disc had a smaller disc in the centre which you could push in, put your finger in the small hole and pull out the large disc to pour the milk. We used to put two of those cardboard discs with a hole together and then wind wool through the centre hole and around the outside edge of the discs. When the winding was finished, we would carefully cut all around the wound wool between the two discs and then tie another piece of wool tightly between them. When you pulled off the discs, you were left with a woollen pom-pom.

Next door to the Co-op dairy was the Co-op grocery shop. It was a lovely old place which smelled strongly of tea and coffee and cheese. The counters and woodwork were all polished mahogany and all along the front of the counter were tin boxes with hinged glass lids, containing things like raisins, currants, biscuits and tea.

The lids could be lifted open so that you could buy the contents loose by weight. The shopkeeper would use an aluminium scoop and plain brown paper bags. No fancy packaging, I often think such practice would make more sense today, rather than the infuriating bubble-wrap and other such fancy packaging equally impossible to open.

All the kids in the area had a veritable playground, right on their doorstep, which led right out into the country. From Wheatley Crescent, where I was born, from Cromwell Road, Monmouth Road, Charter Road and all the other streets in the Lambrook area they came, as well as all the streets in the Halcon area nearby.

One of our favourite areas was Priory Fields where Wickes DIY now stands and beyond, from which we could go all the way out to Bathpool Village via 'Long Fields' as we called them following the river.

Families were very poor in those days and kids had to make their own entertainment.

We would make fishing rods from a bamboo garden cane commonly used for runner bean supports. A large part of the fun was in running around finding the materials and excitedly making the rods.

We would make a series of little holes in the bamboo with a nail and then screw in some curtain eyelets. A cotton reel nailed to the cane with some cotton wound on it was our reel and line, a cork from a bottle, with a lollipop stick through it for a float and a bent pin for a hook.

We would then use a little trick to get some worms for bait, by scrounging some Colman's mustard powder from Mum. It used to come in a little oval-shaped tin about twice the size of a matchbox. We would make a weak mixture of the mustard powder with some water and then put a couple of spoonfuls down a wormhole. After a short wait in anticipation, a worm would shoot out of the hole as if it was on fire. All you had to do then was to grab it and put it into your jam jar, which had some string tied around its neck, with a loop for carrying.

Off we would troop with our rods carried proudly over our shoulders, a jar of worms in the other hand.

I particularly remember one such outing. We noisily decided to fish near a man with all the proper equipment, behind the rugby ground. There he was, sitting on his posh wicker fishing box, an expensive split cane fishing rod, keep net in the water, etc.

He looked distinctly annoyed when the scruffy little bunch of kids settled near him.

With a flick of his wrist, he could easily cast right across the river. We would give an almighty swishing heave of our makeshift rods and the resultant splash would be about six feet out from our side of the bank.

We would then intently watch our little cork floats for an indication of a 'bite', all the time keeping a watchful eye open for the approach of a Water Bailiff. We had no fishing licences and would run for it if we saw him coming.

There was my float drifting lazily along in front of me, when suddenly it vanished beneath the surface. I jerked the rod upwards and feverishly fumbled with the cotton reel. Somehow, I managed to land the most beautiful orange—finned roach I have ever seen. The man near us hadn't caught anything and I swear the back of his neck went red with jealousy and frustration when he saw me catch that beauty with such rubbish fishing equipment.

Whilst writing this book, during December 2001, I noticed some widening work towards the vehicle entrance to what is now the Asda superstore. The excavations revealed some huge blocks of concrete and brickwork. I knew instantly what they were.

I wonder how many other local people realised. The Asda store is actually built on what was once the local tip and I am told that they had to install pipes under it to carry away the methane gas which was or is generated by the rotting buried material. The local boys would often go scavenging at the tip and would carry away things like bicycle frames and wheels and pram wheels, etc. We almost never had any money and we had to make our own entertainment.

I can still remember seeing boys and girls riding around on bikes with no tyres and no brakes either. The bare metal wheel-rims made a very noisy clattering sound. Pram wheels were always good for making what we called trolleys. We would lay the axle on a piece of wood and drive in nails on each side of the axle and then bend the nails over to hold the axle to the wood.

Even the nails were second-hand, we straightened them out by hammering them on the ground. One pair of fixed wheels at the back and one pair at the front of a plank, which we sat on. The front wheels were made steerable by putting an old bolt through for a pivot. The trolley would be completed by nailing a piece of wood to the edge of the plank with one nail so that it could be pivoted and used as a highly ineffective brake, which rubbed on a tyre.

We always referred to the tip as 'the sewage'. There is a particularly sad story attached to the salvaging forays. I remember a boy older than myself, whose name was Philip Batten. He lived with his mum and dad at number 15 and had an older sister called Lavinia. The kids called Philip 'the sewage king', because he was always down there finding stuff and bringing it home. He contracted polio and died, I often wonder if he got that awful disease from the tip.

Just a few yards into Roman Road was and still is the narrow footpath which ran parallel to the filled-in gully. This was what we called Roman Lane. The footpath led right up over the rise, past the end of Moorland Road, then down past the end of Valley Road and on at the back of the Valley Road houses where it led over a little stream and then along the perimeter fence of that mysterious place which we kids knew as 'The Admiralty'.

It was, of course and still is, the United Kingdom Hydrographic Office, where amongst other things, the highly regarded admiralty charts of the world's oceans are made.

The point where the footpath met the stream and the perimeter fence was where the new entrance to the hydrographic office is today. The stream is still there and so is the continuation of the footpath along the fence past the old

Nissen hut, which is also still there. The entrance to the 'Admiralty' at that time was about 100 metres away on another street, at the bottom of Crossways Hill and between two areas of little prefabricated single-storey houses, 'The Prefabs' as we called them.

Anyone venturing down the hill of 'crossways' today will come to the fence and on looking through it, would see a small brick building with a flat concrete roof. This was the original gatehouse for the security men and later became the dog kennel.

The hill has now been fenced off but, in those days, it was possible to get into the field and play.

The hill was a place where kids could play and tumble. There were small terraces in places and molehills, which became very apparent when the hill was used for the favourite pastime of sledging when there was snow. All the local kids would show incredible ingenuity in making sledges in double quick time. I remember seeing all sorts of weird contraptions, like for example, sledge runners made out of car bumpers from the local tip which was nearby and even a sledge made out of a pair of 'borrowed' step ladders.

When you were skimming down the hill on your sledge, a molehill would become very apparent if you hit one buried in the snow. The sledge would suddenly stop and you would continue your forward momentum, face down, head first or on your back feet first until you vanished into a snowdrift at the bottom under the hedge.

I can just remember as a very small child, being taken there by my brothers and sisters. Someone had put socks on my hands to keep them warm as we could not afford gloves. I was too small to take part in the sledging so stood around watching the others for ages. I became very cold and was crying. They took me home and as my hands thawed out by the fire, I was in agony.

I did my growing up whilst living first at 16 Wheatley Crescent, then moving to 28 Cromwell Road and then 25 Charles Crescent. Gradually, my older brothers and sisters married during this time, the first was Betty in 1950. The same year my mum met Norman Goldrick who was from Manchester. She met him at The Labour Club in Priory Bridge Road having divorced my dad 3 years previously. She very soon married him and Barry (my stepbrother) was born the same year. So I now had a stepfather.

Whilst she had Norman and Barry, my brother Brian and his wife would come with their car and take them off to the seaside. No room in the car for me so I would be left at home alone all day to fend for myself.

I used to scrounge off-cuts of wood from any builders doing work and whilst Mum, my stepfather and Barry were at the seaside, I would spend the day making clothes-horses which I would sell to one of our neighbours to get a bit of money.

9 years after marrying my mum, Norman got me a job as an apprentice pattern-maker and I had to leave school at 15 and start that job to begin bringing money in for my keep. I was in the sixth form at school and wanted to 'stay on' to get some qualifications, but was told I had to get a job.

I started work as an apprentice pattern-maker in 1959, my stepfather got the job for me without my knowledge until he announced it to me, I think he must have known Mr Poole who became my first boss. It was quite possible because he worked in a scrap metal yard at the time and I now know that

Mr Poole used to sell scrap bronze turnings from his lathes. Whilst I was employed there, dealers did come to collect swarf from the lathes.

Below, is the grocery shop, which was owned and run by Mr Poole (Senior) and his wife. The son of these people was Des Poole, who had his pattern-making workshop in the garden behind the shop. So we all went through the door beside the shop, down the alley with our bicycles each morning.

I worked very hard there for a few years as something of a dogsbody, to begin with, but did learn some useful wood and metalworking skills. Patterns are used to make moulds for castings and so pattern-making is a very skilled trade.

We were so 'hard up' as apprentices, that another one called Pete Bellamy and I would club together the few pence we had and buy 5 Woodbines. We would have 2 each and wrestle until one of us submitted for the remaining one.

I constantly thought about trying to find some kind of work which I could enjoy more and which would benefit society and make things better for poor people like us, so I could draw some kind of reward from it. This was to be my mission in life because I wanted to help change the inequality that existed between the 'working-class' and the 'privileged', having experienced such austerity.

My brother Colin married in 1960.

Then at work one day, a guy called Mike Gibbs (an electrician) came into our workshop and started wiring up a new lathe. I was intrigued to see that it had to have red, yellow, blue, black and green cables as well as loads of grey ones. I spoke with him and he explained that it was a 3-phase machine with loads of control wires.

I was very interested and after thinking about the fact that everyone has to have electricity, I decided that I wanted to be an electrical engineer, because by getting involved in that I would have a huge chance to have an effect on everyone in the community and would probably have a 'Job for Life'.

When Norman died, my mum decided to take Barry and move in with my brother Brian and his wife just down the road, the same ones who used to leave me at home when they all went off to the seaside.

There was no room for me so I had to go and live with my sister Betty and her husband and children for some years at their house in crossways.

I had already experienced much poverty, hardship and unfairness. Whilst at secondary school, for example, my school friend Dave was the son of the manager of Taunton Lipton's Tea Shop. We would often go to the shop after school and I very distinctly remember looking in wonderment at the loads of Tea Chests out the back with their stencilled marks.

'Produce of Ceylon', 'Broken Orange Pekoe Fannings' and 'Colombo', etc. (Ceylon is now Sri Lanka), which strangely later became a place I loved.

Dave never equalled me at school, but when we both passed the 13-plus exam (me with a higher mark than he), he was given a place in Huish Grammar School and I believe I was denied a place because all I had was a stepfather who was a labourer in a scrap metal yard. My school friend Dave went on to become the owner of a Taunton Estate Agents and became the chairman of the National Association of Estate Agents.

Priory Secondary Modern School on Cranmer Road, Priory Junior School is at the far end of the road to the left of the trees.

****

It's another slightly strange fact, that I went to St James School at age 3, became a choirboy at St James Church whilst at secondary school and began my electrical career at St James Street.

I believe St James was the first Apostle to be martyred for his beliefs.

Next to marry were Beryl and Tony in 1951. King George 6th died on 14 Dec 1952 and Mum married Norman in 1953, the same year that Princess Elizabeth was crowned Queen. I took part in a coronation kids' sports day at The Labour Club and was given an orange and a coronation mug. My brother Brian married in 1955, Jillarie in 1957.

For a few years before leaving school, I had a job delivering newspapers for W. H. Smith. I was paid 10 shillings per week (which is 50 pence today).

It stood next door to today's Lloyd's Bank and is now a Topshop branch.

In about 1957, one morning I went to the shop to get my papers for delivery and the shop had partially collapsed just before I arrived. They were excavating the vaults for the new Lloyds bank and must have caused Smiths to subside.

There was a long narrow passageway down the left-hand side of the shop which led to the back of the shop and a room where all the paper rounds were made up into a bundle for each delivery boy. The right-hand wall of the passageway had collapsed against the left-hand wall. If I had been walking down it at that moment, I would have been crushed, I was very lucky indeed.

The collapsed W.H. Smith building.

I left my employment as an apprentice for two reasons: One was that my girlfriend at that time was the daughter of a lady who owned 'The Bonaventure Café' in Upper High Street, Taunton. They were moving to Torquay and I went with them. I suppose you could say I had 'dropped-out'. I hoped to get some kind of electrical employment (my other reason) down there but this never materialised.

My ex-boss (Mr Poole) was not a very nice man at all when I told him I was leaving. He absolutely refused to give me any kind of reference or letter stating that I had completed a large part of my apprenticeship with him and his little company. I needed that from him in case I had to revert back to similar work and could continue my apprenticeship with someone else.

After all the profit he had made from my hard work, he gave me nothing at all. My reward was zero. As an apprentice, I was only paid about £2.50 a week.

Would you believe it, I actually worked for a while for a private detective agency in the Torquay area and my job was 'shadowing' people and going into the same nightclubs and so on, to observe and report back on them.

When my girlfriend and I parted, I went home to my mum at Wellsprings and she understandably said, "You'd better get yourself a job."

I plucked up the courage and went down to the SWEB (now Western Power) main offices on Priorswood Road and asked at reception if there were any job opportunities. The lady rang someone and said a Mr Ken Atherton (Initials K. A., same as mine) was coming down to see me. He met with me and invited me to his office.

He said that there were not currently any jobs advertised but he admired my enterprising approach. I had told him of my new interest in electrics and wanting to work with something which benefits everybody. He just so happened to be SWEB's head of electrical engineering.

He said he was prepared to take me on as an 'Improver', which was a new idea they were thinking of introducing. He warned me that I would have to be prepared to do hard, heavy work in some departments because he would be putting me with cable layers, overhead line gangs, cable jointers and electrical fitters, etc., to get me acquainted with all aspects of electrical distribution. He also said I would have to go to college.

I eagerly accepted and began working from their St James Street Depot one week later.

I was put with a cable laying gang and it was a very rude awakening for me. I had to dig trenches with all the other guys using picks and shovels and pneumatic breakers.

I went home the first day with bleeding blisters on my hands and fell asleep over my dinner. I began to get used to the hard work of trenching and pulling in 3-ton drums of cable. It certainly toughened me up though!

After a while, he transferred me onto an overhead line gang. We had to dig pole holes, erect the poles, climb the poles and fit arms and insulators, erect pole-mounted transformers and string the cables from pole to pole and connect it all up.

I very distinctly remember one particular job we did on Exmoor in harsh winter conditions. We were tasked with bringing electricity to the famous little Oare Church on Exmoor for the first time. Oare Church is where Lorna Doone (a famous book written by R. D. Blackmore) was supposedly almost fatally shot at the altar by her half-brother Carver Doone as she married John Ridd.

From the last pole, we had to take the cable underground across the back graveyard and up into the church. We could not dig a trench without disturbing the graves so we dug two pits, one at the foot of the pole outside the wall of the church grounds and one near the rear window through which Lorna was reputedly shot.

We used a hydraulic thrust-borer to drive a ram underground from one pit to the other and then pulled the cable through the hole it had created. Lord only knows what that ram head went through on the way.

Believe it or not, I actually found a brass cartridge about 12mm in diameter with a little brass pin sticking out of the rim in the spoil from the pit near the church wall.

It had been discharged so there was no ball!

I am so very annoyed, because somehow I lost it years ago.

Apparently, pin fire was a cartridge type patented in the 1830s and so it just could fit the scene because Blackmore wrote the novel in 1867.

I seem to remember some of us putting our names in the Church Visitors Book as South-Western Electricity Board employees who installed the electricity supply.

I believe the church had to use a harmonium-type instrument, which had air pumped to its pipes by foot pedals until we installed the supply.

It could obviously then have an electric organ as well as lighting, etc.

Oare Church on Exmoor.

After more time, Ken Atherton put me with cable jointers and my digging was over.

He then promoted me to Fitter's Mate and I began attending college. Over time, I eventually did 72 exams (including 'phase-tests').

The 'poor boy', who had been refused a grammar school place, eventually got all his qualifications through further education.

We were installing switchgear and transformers in substations, etc. Ken Atherton then told me to go and have driving lessons and the SWEB would pay me back whatever it cost if I brought him the receipts.

So I enrolled with the Imperial School of Motoring and was taught to drive by a woman.

She was actually very good and taught me 'Defensive Driving' right from the start.

When I walked back from the driving test centre, my foreman said, "Did you pass?" I said yes and he said, "Right, I've got a job for you." He said, "Take that Land Rover, I want you to go to Barnstaple Quay substation and do some switchgear meter readings."

I had just passed my test and suddenly found myself all alone, proudly driving a 3-litre long wheelbase Land Rover with its SWEB Logos down into North Devon.

I absolutely loved it and went on to become part of a 4-man team upgrading all the high voltage substations around the Westcountry.

Ken Atherton came to see me and said, "Well done, lad—I knew you would make it."

He then shook my hand and told me he was leaving for New Zealand where he had landed a job in charge of their hydro-electrics.

I am forever indebted to that man for giving me such a chance.

Working on 33,000 volts overhead busbars (me on the ladder) and the indoor equipment which protected it. From faults and lightning.

Unfortunately, after not many years of working for the SWEB, I was confronted with redundancy or re-deployment because we had literally worked ourselves out of a job, having done all the necessary upgrading. I took the redundancy and got myself a job in Bridgwater at a small factory called Sidem International which was making shotguns and modifying handguns for the American market.

I was working at the gun factory in Bridgwater as a short-term job.

They employed me to connect up some new machines they were bringing in. I only stayed there for a matter of months.

I then left the gun factory and then moved to another Bridgwater company called EDF Electrical where they manufactured DC starters and other equipment involving windings. I stayed there for about six or seven months.

As our wedding day approached, we both changed our jobs again, Gill going to work in a headquarters building for Debenhams where she was an invoice clerk and myself starting at an electrical manufacturing company in Highbridge.

I had seen an advert for a job at a company called Dynamics, which was making control panels. I got the job of wiring them. One of the panels was about a 20-foot-long assembly of cubicles the size of wardrobes for the Whitgift Shopping Centre in Croydon and another was a control desk for a man operating a gantry crane carrying crucibles of molten iron at the South Wales Steelworks. Needless to say, it had a 'Dead Man Pedal' so everything would stop automatically if his foot came off the pedal.

In 1969, I met Gillian, who would later become my wife. I met her in the Camelot Club, which was situated in the present-day Canon Street Car Park, Taunton. She was working as a dental receptionist/nurse in the town of Wellington.

I left Dynamics in 1970 and started working for a company called Turriffs for much higher pay. This, though, meant living out of a suitcase and working all over the country carrying out conversion from town gas to natural gas.

I had to go on a course at Baginton Aerodrome in Coventry and then worked in places like Cheltenham and Coventry and then we moved down to the south coast where I worked in Seaton, Sidmouth, Exmouth and Honiton.

Gill, as I called her, changed jobs to work at a tailoring firm called Egerton-Burnetts, in Wellington for a short while and then left in August 1971 and went to work as an invoice clerk for Debenhams at their offices opposite County Hall in Taunton.

We had married on 30 July 1971 and moved into a privately rented little bungalow in the Hamlet of Hele, between Taunton and Wellington. Its name was 'The Bungalow' at Syles Orchard and it was of wooden construction with a galvanised iron roof.

I had a 0.410 shotgun hung above the fireplace and Gill was quite scared being there on her own in the almost total darkness surrounding the place, so when I went to night school (college), I used to tell Gill if anyone tried to get in, in the darkness fire the shotgun through the door that'll put 'em off.

My shotgun was a present to me from my good Polish friend named Joe Psyk, who worked as a toolmaker at Dynamics in Highbridge. Joe was a guy who had escaped from a German prison camp in Poland. His profession had been a gunsmith, but he was captured by the Germans whilst he was serving in the Polish army. The German officers at the camp got to know of Joe's gunsmith skills and he maintained their hunting guns for them. He became trusted to the extent that they would let him go with them on their hunting trips in the forest.

Apparently, they each had a 0.410 shotgun with 'over and under' twin barrels. The second barrel was a 0.22 rifle which was very handy, especially if they ran into a wild boar which can be very dangerous. One day they made the mistake of letting Joe go hunting with just one officer. Joe shot him in the leg and made his escape to England.

****

Our intention was to live in the bungalow until we could get a council house in either Taunton or Wellington, but by a strange irony, we could not be considered for either town because we had chosen to live in an area between the two and were now under a separate council authority. This meant that because neither of us now worked in or lived in our towns of birth, we were ineligible.

We soon came to the conclusion that we would have to save hard and try to buy a little house. Whilst living there, our landlord named Redman, lived in Tiverton and he was a devious sort of man. We often suspected that he had duplicate keys and had been snooping around the bungalow whilst we were out at work.

Several times during our tenancy he raised our rent and we eventually came to suspect he was trying to get us out. I now know that he wanted to sell the property to a developer.

Towards the end, he alleged that we were not paying the rent but, in fact, he was not paying in the cheques we sent him.

We consulted a solicitor for what was to prove to be the first but certainly not the last time we would need such professional services.

Mr Michael Rose (solicitor and county coroner) of the Wellington Practice of the impressive sounding name of Messrs Clarke, Willmott and Clarke was our man.

He sent letters to our scoundrel of a landlord which seemed to do the trick and kept him at arm's length.

I worked overtime when I could and we saved hard. Our decision to buy a house was a necessity in our eyes. Our eighteen months at the bungalow were quite pleasant apart from the problems with the landlord, plus the usual disasters that seem to happen during the early part of marriage.

I had an old Triumph Vitesse car and every morning, would drop Gill off at my mum's house at 34 Bagborough Road at Wellsprings Estate in Taunton. From there, Gill would go by bus to work and I would drive on to work in Highbridge, some 18 miles from Taunton. I would collect Gill from my mum's on the way home from work.

One morning, I had dropped off Gill at my mum's and set off for Highbridge as usual. I had only gone about a mile when a paper boy on his bicycle shot out from nowhere right in front of me. It was at the beginning of the hill in front of Priorswood shops.

Fortunately for him, I braked and swerved to the left, narrowly missing him. I was left with insufficient time to stop and my car struck a concrete lamppost on the little island with a grass verge. The lamppost was knocked down and my car was badly smashed up. I actually hit my head on the windscreen. I clambered out and shouted after the boy, who was making off in panic.

A guy who had seen what happened ran after him up the hill and over the crest. I went across the road to the library and asked them if I could use their telephone because my car was un-driveable. They refused to let me call for help. Meanwhile, the guy who had chased the boy came back with the boy's parents and told me their address. They basically didn't want to know.

I got my car towed away and couldn't get to work so I went to see my bank manager at National Westminster Bank. I told him what had happened and as I had very little money in my account, he said, "We must get you to work, so go and buy a little car and write a cheque for it. I will cover it."

I went and bought myself a second-hand blue Mini and was mobile again. My insurers could get nothing from the boy who caused the accident, saying he was a minor. They sent me a settlement for my written-off car after about 3 weeks and I dutifully went to see my bank manager again after paying the cheque in. I asked him how much he would charge me for being overdrawn for 3 weeks. He said, "I am going to charge you nothing. It is my pleasure to help you out."

I have never forgotten that kind gesture and have stayed with that same branch all my life. I have repaid them with my loyalty. I honestly don't believe there would be any such gesture in today's greedy world.

I remember one amusing little incident whilst Gillian and I were living at the bungalow. I was working on my car one weekend morning out in the little outbuilding which served as a garage when I heard a scream. Gillian had got up about an hour after me and began ironing some washing I had brought in from the clothesline. I had unwittingly folded a bat into the pile of washing which I had left in a pile for her. Obviously, when she came to the bat entangled in the laundry, it had freed itself and was flying up and down in our front room.

In May 1972, Gill began a new job at Priory Service Station in Priory Avenue as a manageress.

In the same year, I saw an advert for jobs with BT and applied for it. I was absolutely delighted when I received a letter telling me that my application had been successful and that I was to report to a Mr Meaker at Telephone House, The Crescent in Taunton. I told them of my previous experiences in the electrical field and Mr Meaker said they wanted me to train as a technician and to start by installing telephones in new customers premises to meet the huge demand they had at the time. He did say though, that I would certainly be considered for any future vacancy in their electrical sections.

I began (on 20 March 1972), as a Technician 2B and was put with a guy called Reg Hector, to assist him and 'learn the ropes', so to speak. I went on a training course in Shirehampton, Bristol and was 'in-digs' whilst there.

At a BT Training Course, Shirehampton, Bristol. I am 5th from the left, back row.

The Big House near the top centre was a BT College at Shirehampton, Bristol, with its car park and field.

By a strange coincidence, the bungalow immediately below the college's green door would become the one I 'freelanced' at many years later for my sister-in-law.

The BT College entrance in Shirehampton, High Street, Bristol.

Very soon, I was given a van and started working on my own installing telephones.

With that came a promotion to Technician 2A. After a couple of years, a vacancy arose in the Power Construction section which did all the wiring and electrical work in telephone exchanges and radio stations all over the Westcountry. I applied for the job and got it as they had promised with my previous electrical experience. Now I was in my element.

In January '73, we managed to buy a little terrace house in Wellington at 41 North Street for £4,100 using a mortgage from Wellington Urban District Council.

We 'did the house up' by installing a new kitchen, a central heating system and an upstairs bathroom, etc.

I found an old bread oven embedded in clay in the chimney breast whilst renovating the house and I donated it to Taunton Museum.

Things were gradually becoming brighter for us and we sold 41 North Street for £8,400 and bought our 3-bedroom End of Terrace House at No 11 Leslie Avenue in Taunton. We bought it for £12,500 with a mortgage from Cheltenham & Gloucester Building Society and moved in on 19 October 1978.

After a relatively short time, the foreman of BT's Power Construction Section retired and my boss wanted someone to replace him. He asked around but no one wanted the extra responsibility except me and I gladly accepted it when he offered it to me. Again, it meant promotion and I became a Technician 1.

Only one man in our department now had a higher rank than me as a Technical Officer and he worked almost like a law unto himself and answerable only to our boss. His name was Tom Houkes and his job was a one-off, installing all the diesel generators and AC and DC power plants in the exchanges, etc. Tom (like me), was a meticulous college goer and ended up getting himself a job in Bournemouth working for the council there.

I had been working with him as his assistant for quite some time and became well-acquainted with the work he did so when he left, I was the natural candidate to take over his duties.

My boss gave me the job and all I needed was to go on a course in Iron Acton to learn how to do various kinds of welding.

The following picture shows me working on a new exhaust system I had built and welded for the diesel generator at Burnham on Sea Telephone Exchange when a first-floor Mansard type extension was put onto the previously flat roof and the photo after that is of a diesel generator and me at Taunton 'Toneside' Telephone Exchange.

Installing the new generator exhaust system up onto the new Mansard roof at Burnham Telephone Exchange.

The diesel generator at Taunton Toneside Telephone Exchange and me.

The alternator I am leaning on weighs 7 tons. See the turbocharger beside my head and the exhaust above it, which is 14 inches (35.5 cm) in diameter.

Becoming a bit more prosperous, Gillian and I began taking holidays abroad and our first was a trip to Romania in 1981. This was a roaming exploration of some very interesting places such as Bran Castle (known as Dracula's Castle).

In 1982, we did a tour of Italy, visiting Verona, Venice, Assisi (of the famous St Francis), Rome, Pompei, Sorrento and Capri.

In 1983, we visited Morocco and Gibraltar.

In 1984, we visited the Greek Island of Crete and also Paris the same year.

In 1985, Crete again.

In 1986, we visited Egypt and did a 600-mile Nile Cruise, visiting many of the temples such as Karnak and Luxor, The Valley of the Kings and, of course, The Pyramids. I feel very privileged to have actually been to Tutankhamun's Tomb and in the King's Chamber of The Great Pyramid.

In 1987, we visited Malta.

We had to miss part of 1988 because I had a 'slipped-disc' in my back.

But we still managed to visit Northern Cyprus and spent a couple of weeks exploring it in a jeep I had hired.

In 1989, I had to have an operation on my spine to have the 4th Lumbar Disc removed. It kept me 'off-work' for five and a half months, but we still managed to visit Acapulco on the Pacific side of Mexico.

In 1990, we visited The Dominican Republic in The Caribbean and stayed at an 'all-inclusive' place called 'Club Escapade'.

In 1993, we visited Turkey.

In 1994, we visited Tunisia.

In 1995, we visited Goa, India.

After that, our favourite place became Sri Lanka which we visited 3 times and made many great friends there.

My beloved wife Gillian and I at The Panoramic Hotel in Acapulco, Mexico.

****

Also in August 1990, we began renting a garage just up the road from us whilst we were living at Number 11 Leslie Avenue.

The chap who owned the garages was an ex-colleague of mine whilst I had been employed by SWEB and we eventually (in December) bought the land and garages from him and applied for Outline Planning Permission to build a house there.

I have learned from experience that building your own house can be an exciting and wonderful adventure, culminating in a great and enduring sense of achievement. That, of course, is exactly what it is and should be.

Let no one be in any doubt though, it does mean a lot of very hard work and lots of running around and organising, unless your intention is to leave all that to an expensive architect, for example. So part of this book is about our venture, which in fact went horribly wrong, but turned out well in the end.

It is not my intention to 'put off' anyone considering buying a bit of land and building their own house. Some may be somewhat horrified by what happened to us but hopefully, they will see the possible pitfalls which befell us and will avoid them by learning about from our mistakes.

We had purchased the land for £32,000 between No 20 and 21 Leslie Avenue in December 1990 by using part of our own money and borrowing the rest on our Eagle Star Endowment Mortgage. The land had 6 garages, a store room and an office, the fellow renting the store and office was selling paper bags from there to local stores.

After all the garages and buildings were vacated, I advertised the 6 x sectional concrete garages for sale/buyer to dismantle. I received bids for them and eventually was paid £3,000 for them and they were taken away, leaving only their concrete bases in evidence. This helped by getting us back some of the purchase money and sort of reducing the cost to £29,000.

We applied for and got planning permission for a 4-bedroom detached house on our land and to demolish the office and store and replace them with a brick workshop.

The only conditions were that we had to have off-road parking (a garage) and they wanted to know why we wanted the workshop the size of 3 garages.

I replied that we were only replacing the office and store and that the building was for my Dinghy (which I never had).

Permission was granted and we got a 'stages' mortgage from Cheltenham & Gloucester Building Society. This meant that we would get money from them as we reached stages such as damp course level, first-floor level and so on.

My nephew approached us and said he would build it for us.

His building firm was called Oakshield Developments. Little did we know that he was struggling financially and basically conned us into accepting his quote.

We gave him some money and he started the work after my mother-in-law's friend Tom Holding and I had demolished the old office and store.

One of his sub-contractors was a really nice guy called Trevor Abel who arrived with his Caterpillar Excavator and he quickly broke up the 6 garage bases and began excavating the foundation trenches. Because the site was situated between two rows of 10 terrace houses which only have shallow foundations, the building inspector made us dig the foundations about 5 feet deep until the digger hit hard rocky ground.

The inspector then said, "I want the trenches filled with concrete to form a retaining wall to prevent the adjoining houses from subsiding."

This meant we had to pour 620 tons of concrete into the trenches to fill them.

We discovered that a 9-inch sewer ran under the centre of what was to become our house. Wessex Water Authority insisted that we would have to form 3 new manholes and a 60-foot-long section of new 9-inch sewer pipe to divert it to run under our new garage. This cost us £3200 but after arguing our case about their sewer on our land, serving 10 houses upstream of us, they finally agreed to sign a Legal Agreement with us that they would be liable for all future sewer maintenance and repair.

Work proceeded and the brickwork got to the first-floor level. Then it all suddenly stopped and the bombshell hit us. my nephew said, "I have run out of money and can't get up to roof level," although he had been paid for up to that stage.

We couldn't get any more money until it reached that level and, in desperation, borrowed £6500 and gave it to him. Still, no more work was done and he explained that he had paid it into his bank and it had been swallowed up by his overdraft.

We were forced to cancel the contract with him amid much animosity, etc. and our solicitors were chasing each other about it, claiming that our verbal contract was a much higher figure than we had actually agreed upon.

My nephew and his father actually came to the site and took away bricks, etc., they said they had bought.

I had the NHBC inspector check out the work done so far and he 'failed' some of it, saying some of the new walls were misaligned and that it would be impossible to put a roof on the house.

Meanwhile, the scaffolding company manager approached me and said the hire fee had not been paid. We ended up paying them.

I engaged another builder to put the faults right and realign the walls by taking them down and rebuilding them, after discovering that Local Builders Merchants were also owed money and would not supply materials to our site. I actually had to go round to them all and explain what had happened and to tell them that although my name is Adams, I am not my nephew who owes you money. I agreed with them that I would pay cash for all my orders to show good faith.

Incidentally, I wrote a little poem about our house build and my nephew (the so-called builder) in 1994.

Bless This House

The scaffold towered all around like accusing iron fingers
They seemed to say "It's all gone wrong" and "That is why it lingers."

The firm that owned the scaffolding approached us with a frown
Said the Builders Hire has not been paid so you pay money down
It hadn't even reached the stage where funds could be released
The mortgage people said "No more" until the value has increased
We had to borrow money and hand it to him
He paid the lot into his bank and it vanished at their whim
They said he had an overdraft and it paid his deficit,
So he still had no money and couldn't get on with it
The rain ran down like tears inside and moss grew on its walls
So it could give no welcome inside its roofless halls.
And then a tiny gleam of hope came from the darkness thither

From one who said he'd carry on and I, refused to let it wither.
Some of the walls were wrongly built, they just did not align
It wasn't possible to fit a roof, a very ominous sign

Their shoddy work was taken down and carefully rebuilt
This time with proper Craftsmen, experienced to the hilt.
A roof it had and on things went, though sweat and blood was spilt
And floors and stairs and everything, inside its walls were built.
New tradesmen same officials, to it came and went
And everything was passed at last, like something heaven—sent.
As all can see, it rose again, like a phoenix from the ashes
And now has doors and glass in place, all fitted in their sashes.

For twenty-six years, it now has kept the elements at bay
And shelters under its broad roof, those who inside choose to stay.
A fire now flickers in its hearth, in kitchen boils a kettle
Like mother bird under whose wings, it comforts those who settle.
We proved our case before the court and they were ordered to pay our due
So they made it a 'shell company' which made them hard to sue
So they prospered by robbing us and never paid us back
They still demonstrate no conscience and never seem to crack

It is a strong and proud house now in spite of those who lied
But it needs the love of those it shields, for its-The House
that almost died

By: Ken Adams, 10 November 1994.

(Who bought this land called Connaught Garages in 1990,
built this house and moved in for Christmas 1992)

The land for our new house, showing 3 of the old garages and the
Victorian gas streetlight we purchased.

Building it!

The finished new Number 20A Leslie Avenue, as we moved-in in 1992.

The house now, since the addition of PVC double-glazing and fascias, white garage door and purpose made spear-topped gates and railings.

After my dear Gillian died in October 2005, it is true to say that I was in a very sorry state.

I believe anyone with a heart would be, after losing the best thing that ever happened to them in their entire life.

It is an experience that is not comparable in any way with relatively minor things like a divorce, for example.

It is my hope that what follows will paint a different picture of the person I am.

As opposed to the person some people might think I am.

I had been regularly visiting Gillian's mother called Mary whilst Gillian was in hospital. She had been living as a widow in her flat until Gillian's younger sister Helen moved in with her.

The past year at the time of writing has been one of continuing the struggle. The bottom line is that no one in the NHS has been able to come up with any definitive diagnoses of Helen's problems. If they have, then it seems they don't know what to do or cannot do what needs to be done under the remit of the NHS. I am fully committed to finding ways forward though, via other means if necessary. This is actually happening at the moment, anyway.

I find it very strange that no one in our family seems to fully grasp how very, very debilitating Helen's health problems are. I don't think she has anything which is life-threatening, but her levels of pain, etc., are so great that she actually doesn't have a life.

She has great difficulty even just going to a local shop, so going to Totnes for her appointment every month to see the Harley Street Specialist is an ordeal for her. She has missed the last two appointments.

Helen has constant abdominal pain and constant jaw, head and neck pain.

She cannot sleep properly with it. It never gives her a break.

The psychologist she was seeing wrote to her GP saying he could not help her out of her Clinical Depression until her pain levels could be brought under control.

****

(I wrote this quite a while ago, seems appropriate here.)

The Long Tunnel of Adversity

This tunnel is the one that only has one door
And it's one that slams behind you
When your general health is poor
You suddenly lose all the light
And know you can't go back
Your heart then fills itself with fear
In this artificial night
You must walk on through the darkness
And keep to the belief
That a tiny chink of light will come
And you will get relief
That tiny chink of light WILL come
And you will feel a surge
The light will grow bigger, brighter—then
You'll know you will emerge.

****

Wheatley Crescent where I was born, is within a stone's throw of the hydrographic office and on the date given, was actually still employed at the establishment, with the official title of Plant Engineer Electrical and thought that this would probably be the last employment I would ever have at the age of 57.

I began this employment in July 1995 when I left British Telecom after over 23 years.

What a stupid move I had made! I had an enviable job with Telecom; it entailed travelling all over the beautiful west country and working in telephone exchanges and radio stations, etc. I was actually presented with a framed and personally signed valedictory letter by the chairman of BT Sir Ian Vallance, thanking me for my contribution to the company.

The conditions of BT employment were deteriorating, though as a result of privatisation.

When I asked for voluntary redundancy, they did not initially want me to leave, but I talked them into letting me go.

Upon joining the hydrographic office, I very quickly learned what an outdated and old-fashioned establishment it was and contrary to the true traditions of the Admiralty and the Navy, to which it has close links, there were some very bad attitudes present, which I would term as 'them and us'.

It very soon became apparent that 'blue-collar' workers were looked down upon by some of their white-collar managers. I still wonder with disbelief how some of these people got their jobs. They were incompetent and must have got their positions from having been in the services or something. I believe that many of them had 'blagged' their way in or by knowing someone who had served in the forces in their unit.

The main business of the hydrographic office is the production of the world-famous 'Admiralty Charts'. I was employed within a support branch. I shall not mention names or the actual department name, but feel very sure that anyone who was employed in that department at the time and happens to read this will know who I mean.

The 'Hydrographic' is regarded as a prestigious place to work and I have to say, in all fairness, that the huge majority of staff and what they produced were outstanding.

I, though, had unknowingly picked the one department that had incompetent and ruthless managers. In a nutshell, I had unwittingly made the worst career move of my life.

I soon learned that our branch managers were very numerous. Our department had about six managers for about twenty people.

There is no way that so many highly paid managers would be employed to manage so few, in the outside industry, especially such incompetent ones. I guess this is one of the ways in which the civil service gets its bad name. There is a saying "Those who can—do the actual work, those who can't somehow get the highly paid job."

The great majority of the staff employed at the establishment enjoyed non-industrial status, but the minority, consisting of a small number of skilled craftsmen including myself, together with a few unskilled workers, were industrials and as such did not enjoy the same conditions of service or levels of pay as their non-industrial colleagues. The situation allowed an unskilled person to be better paid, etc., than a skilled person if he or she was on the right side of the fence (non-industrial).

There was a time when a skilled craftsman was valued in this country.

As a Master Builder, my father was an example of that. What seems evident these days, though, is the fact that there has been neglect by employers in failing to have apprentices to learn skills.

It seems to me, a bitter irony, that there still seems to be something that no one can quite put their finger on, call it an 'old-boys network' or 'if your face fits' or possibly 'something more sinister' if you will, but from what I have seen, there are people in grades they should not have. I have seen very real evidence of incompetent managers enjoying cushy jobs whilst relying heavily on the downtrodden craftsmen they pretend to 'manage'.

These people, in reality, are what I call 'chancers'. They have no appropriate qualifications or knowledge of the work done by their charges and in fact, could not do the job themselves, yet it is they, who get paid the high money when that should be going to the persons who are properly qualified and who can and do actually carry out the work.

This begs the question, how did they get their posts?

The 'chancers', as I call them, are in a position of power. They are in charge and it is they who determine the welfare, prospects and reward of their 'underlings'.

They see themselves as 'the boss'. They have lost sight of the fact that they are not bosses at all, they are employees, just like their charges and they have a duty to treat everyone fairly and support their staff.

They also have a duty as Civil Servants, not to waste public money or do anything dishonest or corrupt. In practice, from what I have seen, they do just the opposite. Perhaps they are not corrupt, but dishonest and devious, they certainly are.

Furthermore, they get away with it.

When challenged, in any shape or form, by disputes or disagreements and so on, their superiors close ranks and back them up with such statements as "I have every faith in my managers." The poor old underlings are thus condemned to struggle without resolution of their problems, whilst the 'chancers' create even better posts and promotions for themselves.

This, then, is what happened to myself and my colleagues at the hydrographic office.

Over a period of about 3 years, it became clear to us that our managers had been 'bluffing' their way through whilst relying on us and (often, cowboy) contractors.

By means of their crafty manoeuvres, they suppressed the craftsmen by preventing them from getting right and proper grades and also by preventing them from achieving the 'single status' that the M.O.D. wanted all staff to have.

It very much appeared to us that they did this to us craftsmen, basically because they 'feared' us, knowing that we craftsmen were better qualified than they to carry out the required work and to document it properly. The result was that they 'threw money' at contractors.

They were unable to correctly specify and plan jobs for their own staff, so they 'kept us down' by giving us mediocre tasks and kept us at arm's length by not including us in project meetings and the like. When we asked for technical support (knowing they couldn't answer), they would take the work away from us and give it to contractors. The contractors would get away with murder because the managers did not know how to supervise them properly. Then the scenario would arise that the 'in house' staff would be expected to put right the poor work the contractors had done.

When it came to a study of the whole department, by means of JEG (Job Evaluation and Grading), which was looking at the feasibility of transferring many of our jobs to contractors, the managers recommended that they themselves be the staff retained, calling themselves 'The Intelligent Customer' whilst recommending that we their charges, lose our civil service status, in other words, keep the incompetents and get rid of the skilled people. If that is not twisting things and wasting public money, then I don't know what is.

I believe the situation there was well summed up by the old Arab proverb which rings very true: "Never cast your pearls before swine."

Our jobs were evaluated by an external agency and we should have ended up with fewer managers, proper grades for the skilled craftsmen, etc., but our managers manipulated the outcome to suit themselves. They gradually reduced our capabilities by removing and selling off our machinery, giving us smaller workplaces and making a few of our assistants redundant.

Over a period of time, we were made to share computers when we needed our own to properly maintain our databases, etc. Generally just making things very difficult for us. One of my colleagues, 'saw the writing on the wall'. He studied at college and got himself a better job elsewhere. I got very stressed-out by the treatment I was subjected to and ended up walking out of the place, never to return.

On a more positive note, though, I was given a very good reference for prospective future employers by a certain Lieutenant Commander RN (of another department), for whom I had done much work. He was a shining example of the many very good people employed there and I will state once more that such people were in the majority. I unfortunately became ensnared under the bad few.

My colleague had 'seen the light' and studied meticulously at college to get himself out of the dreadful department and into a new post as a Mapping and Charting Officer.

I was now working alone, with my colleague gone and both of our assistants having been made redundant.

The manager who had basically been bullying me then turned ever more aggressive in his attitude towards me. He deliberately made things very difficult for me by making me relocate my Electrical Workshop to a totally inadequate, smaller place.

He 'rubbed-it-in', so to speak, by making me do all the rewiring, etc., to turn my previous workshop into a far too big 'First Aid Post'.

He had my computer removed by the IT department and so I lost access to all the electrical test records which I was supposed to maintain and check.

I had to use the computer in the carpentry workshop to do my time sheets, etc.

In the end, he tried to make me leave my job in many devious ways and finally, I took all my own personal tools to my car and left one evening, never to return.

I went to see my doctor the next morning and he 'signed me off sick' because he could see the stress I was being subjected to.

In this way, I managed to get my holiday pay, etc., which even though he had tried to deny me.

So now, here was I without a job and had to decide, where do I go from here?

I began freelancing by doing electrical jobs for various people, in and around Taunton. Things like house rewires and other such works. I had accounts with several electrical wholesalers and soon became fairly established with sufficient work and income to see me through.

I was also able to go to auctions more with my wife Gillian. We would take our transit van, which I had purchased from BT and buy electrical appliances like cookers and washing machines.

I would thoroughly test and check them over, doing any repairs necessary and then Gillian would sell them as part of her little self-employed business.

Very soon though, my brother-in-law Alan approached me and wanted me to do quite a big project in Bristol for his wife Sheila, who was starting up a business which supplied carers to people who were funded by the NHS.

She had purchased a large Maisonette-type bungalow at Shirehampton in Bristol and wanted to convert the large living room to a training room, the bedrooms to accommodation for live-in carers and the first-floor to offices for about 8 or 10 people. I did all the re-arrangements of the electrics, etc. I also converted a part of the large garden into a car park for her staff. I used my own compressor and sprayed the whole bungalow a different colour on the outside.

One hot summer day, I went upstairs to the offices to make myself a refreshing cup of tea (which I could do anytime I wanted one). I was dressed in my one-piece overalls with the front buttons undone, revealing my hairy chest. I was quite sweaty in my overalls on such a hot day but had to wear them. As I walked past the office girls with my cuppa, one of the girls growled "RRRRRRR" at my appearance. Quite good for my ego!

In all, I must have been working there for somewhere approaching 2 years.

Then I saw an advertisement in our local *Somerset County Gazette* newspaper.

Taunton Deane Borough Council wanted to recruit a grants officer and they particularly wanted someone with electrical experience, who was used to liaising with members of the public, contractors and people in many office-type environments.

The advert pointed out that this was to be a 'front-line' post-meeting directly with vulnerable people in the community together with doctors, occupational therapists, contractors and the like. The successful candidate would need to have proof of trustworthiness and knowledge of AutoCAD (the international standard of computer aided design) would be an advantage.

I fitted the bill perfectly, with my South-Western Electricity, British Telecom and M.O.D. electrical pedigree. With both BT and the M.O.D., I was (and still am for life).

A subject of the Official Secrets Act.

I had also done AutoCAD at college so I was able to convince the interviewers that I was their man and got the job on a two-year contract.

What a contrast to the managers at the hydro I found.

On my first day in the Deane House as a local government officer, I began using their AutoCAD software and produced drawings with the 'Taunton Deane' logo on them. They had the software but until now, no one who knew how to use it.

I thoroughly enjoyed working there, it was very rewarding having the authority to design and implement aids, adaptations and installations for disabled people in the community. My manager said in my first 'appraisal', "Ken has brought new levels of skills and expertise to the office and is a valuable member of the team."

My 2-year contract actually lasted for over 5 years until I left to retire.

It was an incredibly friendly place to work, I was on flexi-time and always started early. The CEO would walk into our office and say, "Morning, Ken, early bird again," and she would make me a cup of coffee. What a difference in attitude compared to the incompetent yet arrogant managers at the hydro.

****

I began writing this book quite a long time ago, but on the 12 March 2002, I decided to insert a couple of pages which follow. I believe they are an illustration of the type of dishonesty and greed that seem prevalent nowadays.

There are many who believe this is the legacy of a certain Margaret Thatcher who presided over the greatest con trick in British history.

She sold all the utility companies to the British public, which they already owned.

This was done under the pretext that they would become shareholders with an interest in the company they worked for or owned a stake in. As soon as Joe public sold his shares for a quick buck, they were snapped up by the money-men (Thatcher's cronies). She also made it possible to buy council houses so that 'more people can become homeowners'. Just look at house prices now! I pity the youngsters who struggle to afford a first home and, of course, the 'sold-off' council houses are no longer available to them.

My niece lived in an ex-council flat and the landlord charged her double the rent that she would have to pay in an identical council flat nearby.

I am a great critic of the 'everything has to be run for profit' or 'the free market' approach used by most politicians nowadays.

This has actually resulted in most of our national assets being now owned by foreigners. I believe that this is a road to eventual disaster. It's like a game of *Monopoly*—you end up with one person owning everything.

Over the years, I have come to the conclusion that the so-called 'free market monetarist' practices are leading us entirely the wrong way.

We see 'globalisation' happening. We learn that a very small percentage of the world's population owns about a quarter of the planet. They are billionaires.

To my mind, we only have to ask ourselves the question "Who actually needs billions?" Surely the answer has to be 'no one'!

At the time of writing, I find that our electricity supplier is French-owned, our gas comes from Russia and every time I turn on a tap, someone in Malaysia makes money whilst our local MP (who is currently Environment Minister), signed an agreement with water companies to allow them to dump untreated sewage into our rivers.

What kind of madness is this?

All countries constantly now seem to talk about their 'economy' and their 'national debt', but what are they?

Essentially, the billionaires invest and lend vast sums to make more money for themselves and this trickles all down through what I call 'the system' in which all the various levels below the billionaires make money from all the levels alongside or below them. All this trickles right down to the very bottom level where people exist in abject poverty. These are the people who are exploited the most.

We have all been conditioned to accept that this is normal.

Imagine an upside-down pyramid. A heavy weight presses down on the top and this pressure is widely spread at the top levels, so it is relatively gentle but it gradually increases all the way down through the pyramid until the point of the pyramid is reached. This is the point at which the greatest pressure is exerted by the weight at the top. In other words, the people at this point are the poorest of the poor. That is the way 'The System' works.

The 'national debt' is what the government owes to the money lenders.

The 'economy' is the amount of money received from taxes, revenues, etc., balanced against what is owed to the money lenders.

The Tory government call themselves Conservatives. What exactly is it that they wish to conserve? The answer is: The Tory government gets its party funds in donations from the big money-men.

Corruption is rife!

The big money-men use expensive lobbyists to pressure Tory ministers to vote for what is advantageous to them (rather than vote in the best interests of the people they are supposed to represent—the voters).

So in essence the Tory government exists to maintain the interests of the big money-men and themselves. They also make quite sure that the richest have tax cuts, tax dodges, non-taxable offshore funds, etc.

This is the way in which they maintain the class system, which ensures that the rich are advantaged in every way whilst the poor are disadvantaged, receive a lesser education, are exploited and are heavily taxed.

There is an old saying: "Money goes to money."

I believe this is absolutely true.

All you ever hear about nowadays is corruption and more corruption, oligarchs, business magnates, tycoons, bankers, foreign investors, etc. They are all at the same game—tax dodging, offshore investments, takeovers, selling off our national assets, Swiss bank accounts, lobbying of MPs, etc.

We are all at the mercy of these people, whose only aim is to become revoltingly rich at the expense of all below them and to possess ever more in their insatiable greed.

It is my belief that all this marked the beginning of the end of our once great Island Nation. At the time of writing, we are plagued with high inflation, numerous strikes by workers. Great Britain is what I now see as my second 'Lost Island'.

I am an admirer of Sir Richard Acland, who in 1944 (the year I was born) wrote a book entitled *Unser Kampf* (Our Struggle). Vehemently opposed to capitalism, he was obviously a Christian Socialist and gave his Killerton Estate to the National Trust.

He himself was an admirer of Conrad Noel 'The Red Vicar of Thaxted' who was of like mind.

14 Oct 2020

I have tried to show in this book, the way in which I was born into a family which suffered misfortunes, poverty and disruptions during a time when there was not much help available for the poor and all the things that can follow-on from such a situation to make things hard for those enduring it. Things which appeared to happen as a result of our status and the need to earn money in a world where there is exploitation of the poor and in which there definitely seems to be evidence of an enduring 'class system' which, has boomed to create ever greater disparity since the austerity which followed the Second World War.

The Coronavirus pandemic of 2020 onwards, has given me time to do a bit of extra 'Thinking outside of the box', something I have long enjoyed doing since I made the acquaintance of my late friend Sir Arthur C. Clarke.

There is no doubt in my mind that he changed my way of thinking even though I firmly believe I have always been something of a philanthropist.

Such things as: cosmetics, facades, falsities and misinformation have been in my thoughts.

When you consider such things, alongside things like: evolution, development, industrialisation, technology, etc., you begin to experience fear for the future of mankind.

We now see: population explosion, the destruction of Rainforests going on apace with the approval of Governments who are obviously profiting personally from allowing it. All the natural resources are being depleted and even being used as political weapons (oil, gas, etc.)

It has become my belief that, as a species, we have been conditioned to accept that some of our kind will be very privileged and the rest won't be. It has become accepted that most will never be on a level playing ground and that top jobs, top positions, lavish lifestyles and indulgence are reserved for the relatively few who possess a thing called money. Everyone else, at various levels, are confined to maintaining and preserving that system.

The Victorians are hailed as great innovators and industrialists, but what was their motivation and what did they actually achieve and at what human cost?

They dug canals and built railways, etc., using Navvies. Imagine having to dig a canal by hand using picks and shovels and carts. That is precisely what the Navvies actually did. They worked long arduous hours for meagre pay and the underlying purpose was for the wealthy to sit in their opulent surroundings and watch money pour in without lifting a finger.

The rich sponsors of mining, cotton mills, the railways and basically everything which made fortunes for them were the owners of the great houses which are much admired today by visitors. Why do we admire them? They are actually monuments and symbols of capitalism and exploitation of the poor. My own mother was 'in service' as a scullery maid in just such a great house called Barton Grange.

It actually had 365 windows (the same as days in a year). It was so large that it had entrances from 3 villages (Trull, Pitminster and Corfe) there were lodge houses at each entrance.

Long before them came the feudal system and competition for land, property and the time of peasants, serfs, barons, lords and kings.

The whole thing, when you think carefully about it has always been based upon greed, inequality, exploitation of the poor, selfishness and indulgence.

The East India Company was a well-known business which carried spices, etc., of great value from the far east, so much so, that they had to carry soldiers aboard their vessels to protect their interests. This is how the Marines were created! Men were even press-ganged into becoming crew!

They sought men in drinking dens and clubbed the inebriated ones into unconsciousness. They would wake up with a hangover aboard a ship bound for India.

So the creation of great inequalities by landowners, shipowners and the like, coupled with their exploitation of the poor under their direct and ruthless control, led to the possession of great wealth by a few and poverty for the many.

With the advent of the Victorians, those with all the money invested in mining, cotton mills, railways and many other similar ventures.

Cotton mills for example were in great evidence and they used cheap labour and even children to tend the looms, in conditions of extreme hardships and hard labour.

I have always had an interest in local history and, during my explorations of the Brendon Hills Iron Mines, I saw what looked like a shelf carved into the rock at a point in one of the

Horizontal Adits at Kennisham Hill Mine. It was situated at a right-angle turn in the tunnel where they had turned the heading to follow the iron lode they had intercepted and it was about 2 feet above the floor.

I now know that the little 6-inch 'shelf' was a seat for a boy to sit on in absolute darkness, except for his Tallow Candle which stood on an iron candle bracket hammered into the wall of the rock.

He would have to sit there for about 10 hours a day in the cold and damp, greasing the sharp bend in the rails and helping the iron ore wagons around the corner. In all likelihood, the boy did not get an education, did not live to any reasonable age and probably died of something like tuberculosis.

Incidentally, there is an inscription in the stonework above the entrance to the Old Bailey in London which reads: "Protect the children of the poor, punish the wrongdoer." (Somewhat ironic!)

So what exactly do we glean from such facts? To me, it poses questions!

Why do we admire great houses and their vast estates? They were built by people in possession of great wealth, which was unscrupulously amassed by slave traders, plantation owners, industrialists, shipowners and the like.

Today, it is still inherited wealth and/or ill-gotten wealth that basically runs the lives of all the people on Earth. We are all aware of the oil barons, oligarchs, dictators, Swiss bankers, magnates and so-called entrepreneurs. Almost without exception, they amass huge fortunes through work done by others whilst they sit back and even by unashamed corruption.

If there was any sense in human minds, we would bulldoze the 'great houses', give the land back to the people and confiscate the ill-gotten wealth.

We blindly accept huge estates, private beaches, private woodland, private islands and even a privately owned Lands-End!

What a disgraceful situation! That which mother nature provides is intended for us all, not just the rich. Royal Mail is now privately owned, the water we must have is in private hands.

There are 7 times as many animals for food than there are humans who eat them.

Vast swathes of rainforest are being burnt to make space for even more cattle for us to eat.

We are busily removing all the natural resources from our planet, such as oil, coal, gas, iron, bauxite (aluminium), tin, copper, lead, lithium (for batteries), etc., etc.

This is increasing all the time because of a very simple reason—population explosion fuelled by the constant wants and desires that drive the species called man.

It is all explained, by indulgence in things like drinking, smoking, holidaying, sex, materialistic wants, driving, flying and generally raping the very planet we live on.

The money-men exploit all the foregoing for all their worth to get ever more money and to widen the gap between themselves and ordinary folk. There are now the obscenely rich and all the various other levels beneath them but with an ever-widening gap in the disparity.

Even sport has lost its identity. 'Sport' no longer exists in its true form, it is now all about money.

How can it be right that a Golfer allegedly has £80 million?

How can it be right that a driver allegedly has £40 million?

Chelsea Football Club—owned by a Russian oligarch.

Manchester City—owned by Arabs.

Manchester United—owned by Americans.

All of them use overpaid foreign players to the almost total exclusion of English players.

This situation is what I now call 'The Other Lost Island'—our country!

Why? Because we don't own it anymore, it's largely foreign-owned and controlled by their money!

Either we get ourselves a very different system in which the rich do not run this world of ours but instead, everything is done for the benefit of mankind (not for the rich) and done more frugally and carefully or we are hastening our own doom. That is the stark choice!

The French had the right idea during their revolution. The obscenely extravagant bourgeoisie was epitomised by Marie Antoinette when her scornful remark about the starving peasants was:

"Let them eat cake."

The people quite rightly took her to an appointment with Madame Guillotine at the Place De La Concorde! Right now, the global pandemic is being guided more by 'the economy' than by lives.

Albert Einstein once said, "Only two things are infinite: the universe and man's stupidity."

'They'

They should mend the potholes, they should alter things
They should change the politics and improve everything
They are the ones to blame for everything that's wrong
I'm the one who doesn't bother to protest in a throng
I want to indulge myself and eat more than I need
I conveniently forget that there are hungry mouths to feed.
I fill up all the landfill sites, pollute the sea with plastic
Asking me to put a stop to that, you're being very drastic!
When it comes to voting, I vote for what suits me
I don't vote for what is best for everyone, you see
I drive around regardless, polluting all the air
I indulge myself with holidays because that's only fair
I also indulge myself with cider, wine and beer
It helps me to forget that 'no future' is drawing near
To hell with the legacy, I'll leave the next generation
They will have to sort it out with great determination
There are many poor and many rich and I am in between
The selfish, greedy rich are the ones who set the scene
But I am no better than them 'cause I look after number one

I spend money on myself and just have lots of fun
They should see that businesses like Amazon pay tax
The fact they turn a blind eye is something very lax
The greedy ones lack scruples and they exploit the poor
They don't give to charities when they knock on the door
Although we're all God's children, I don't help others you see
I always have my stock excuse, "That's down to them, not me"
So how about religion? I'll sing in Church and Pray
Then I'll simply wander out and leave the needy down to 'they'.

By: Ken Adams (author), January 2019

I am very proud that the late Sir Arthur C. Clarke always exchanged annual ecograms with me as one of his friends. (It was he who called them that so I copied him and began producing my own annual ecograms).

He used them to tell everyone about his life, his beliefs, his aims, etc., etc.

He did not tolerate fools well and was very critical of greedy people. He was very, very revered by the people of Sri Lanka and they made him a Ramya (a kind of Prince) because he did many good works there for the ordinary people.

I, like Helen, was the youngest of the family. Being the youngest and born quite a few years after the previous child, we both believe we were 'mistakes'.

I, like Helen, never really knew my dad, he left our home when I was very small.

I was born on 30 August 1944, during the Second World War. It was the day the Red Army captured Bucharest and the Ploesti Oilfields in Romania.

****

Thinking about my work over the years, I was in a 4-man team on SWEB that upgraded all the 33,000 volts to 11,000 volts substations in a very large area of the Westcountry.

We basically upgraded all the stations from a capacity of 6-Megawatt output to a capacity of 46-Megawatt output. **This was a huge step in the public interest**, as it would meet the Westcountry's future electricity demands for decades.

Working for BT, I became the only engineer doing my specialised work and covering a huge area from Wincanton to Clovelly. My job was to install and maintain all the power plants that drive all the telephone exchanges and radio stations in that patch.

My power plants are still the reason why the exchanges never stop working even when there is a power cut. All the people of a large part of the west country enjoy vital unbroken communications around the clock. And let's not forget that this is the means of calling doctors, ambulances, police, etc., at any time. On one occasion, BT lent me to the ITV to sort out their plant at Stockland Hill TV station. That's how specialised my work was.

So this was also a work of great importance to the public interest.

Working at the M.O.D.'s Hydrographic Office, my job was to keep all the electrical systems there working. The Hydro runs many operations which protect life at sea, including broadcasting navigational warnings to commercial shipping. It was a routine for one department to test the Short Wave Radio every morning this was a part of North Sea Navigational Warnings. They would say, for example, "Radio Stockholm, Radio Stockholm, Radio Stockholm. This is Uniform Kilo Hotel Oscar, Uniform Kilo Hotel Oscar. How do you read me—over." It meant UKHO—United Kingdom Hydrographic Office.

The Hydro also produces the world-famous Admiralty Charts.

(More work in the public interest).

Working for Taunton Deane as a local government officer, my work involved grants to less well-off people to improve their 'unfit for habitation' homes by tendering and supervising contractors.

I also did much the same for many disabled people by getting disabled facilities constructed for them. Our remit was to enable people to keep their independence and continue to live in their own homes whilst husbanding the public purse. I, personally, had an annual budget of £6.2 million. It was I who planned and executed the job of getting the walk-in shower for Mary. **(More work in the public interest)**

****

I cannot claim to be a religious man, even though I was once a Choirboy at St James Church in Taunton. Events in my life and much travel to various parts of the world, have taught me that Christianity and many other religions, seem to focus on the promise of a life hereafter for the faithful alone. This seems to me to be somewhat selfish of those who seek to achieve it for themselves, to the exclusion of the rest.

I believe that if there is a message for us all, it is that we need to be 'selfless', not 'selfish'! I believe I have always been something of a philanthropist—I have always tried to help others wherever I could.

If any belief has impressed me, I think that it would have to be Buddhism.

I certainly have cause to wonder whether there is such a thing as 'Divine Intervention' or indeed 'Works of the Devil'.

It is in the knowledge that I have always worked in the public interest, my own feelings and things that my friend, the late philanthropist Sir Arthur C. Clarke, taught me, that made me what I am. **He regarded not the theory, but the actual practice of religion as bunk.** Just think for one moment of the Jihadists, for example, who think by killing innocent people in acts of terrorism, they will achieve paradise. That is actually a very selfish thing.

Consider also, for example, what the Catholic Conquistadores did in South America, with their wholesale murder of the people there for their gold. There was also The Inquisition and now, so-called Catholic Christian people treat the Pope as if he is a God!

Not long ago, the Pope allegedly very conveniently forgot to mention the disgraceful abuse of children by 300 Catholic priests in Pennsylvania over the last 70 years.

I actually have Hindu, Muslim and Buddhist friends. The only 'religion' I ever had any respect for was Buddhism. On several occasions, I have had long one-to-one discussions with Buddhist monks sitting under the local sacred Bo tree, as is their custom.

They insist that Buddhism is not a religion but a way of life and that this life is the first one which involves trying to achieve enlightenment through suffering and wisdom if you want to be reincarnated. The Tibetan *Book of the Dead* actually describes the experience of death and guides you to this reincarnation if you are worthy of it.

My interest in Buddhism has now declined somewhat though, since their recent involvement in the Rohingya crisis. It is nothing short of genocide.

To me, one of the most outrageous things in this world at present is the way the world turns a blind eye to the dreadful things the Israelis are doing to the Palestinians. These are the people who are still bringing Nazis to trial whilst themselves, bulldozing Palestinian houses and building settlements for Israelis whilst suppressing the people they are robbing and de-housing with their money and military power.

The world turns a blind eye because of the huge influence of Israeli money in every country of the world. The American President is allegedly no exception.

Sir Arthur C. Clarke considered that there are much more rewarding things to life than the pursuit of money, materialism and self-indulgence. He believed that if there

is anything that could be regarded as 'Christian', it would be that which makes a person selfless and not selfish.

****

Fear, Self and Money

Cars break down you see, 'cause they were made by Man
That's how they try to pass it off, to explain if they can
They go to the scrapyard when they have gone too far
And then you simply go and buy, yourself another car
So why is it that when we die, we don't go to the heap
We are told that when it comes, they say we only sleep
We go to a better place, they say, if that's what we're deserving
Religious folks' belief in this, appears to be un-swerving
The Bible says God copied himself, made us exactly the same
If that's true, then we're able to play his very clever game
Three score years and ten we're told and then it's time for new
We get replaced just like cars, provided we're "One of the few"
Where is this place I ask that we're supposed to go?
When you ask religious folk, they simply do not know
Where is this God they talk about, who we never see
They can't give you an answer, they just have to let it be
If *The Bible* carries a message, then to me it's very clear
Religious folk are selfish, they hold heaven very dear

'Cause they're just thinking of themselves, not others, as you see
They don't follow the teaching, which is "think of they not, thee"
So what is a religious organisation? It's just a money-making plot
That tries hard to convince us that we haven't had our lot
They know that we will be betrayed when the awful truth takes place
They know there's nothing we can do, no need to save their face
We need to accept we won't be saved, by any organisation
We need to know we step aside for the next generation
So stop just thinking of yourself and help others instead
Give these things a little thought before you nestle in your bed.

By: Ken Adams, 1 August 2019

****

I also made another friend of a philanthropist Dutchman in Sri Lanka called Herman Theodorus Steur, who built 'The Netherlands Welcome Village' at Wilagadera.

He actually made his fortune canning seafood in that area **but he didn't spend it on self-indulgence.** He was always a very benevolent man, but one day, a Fisherman's wife and her children came to his house and asked him for help because her husband had drowned whilst out fishing. He was shocked and became aware of the plight of many elderly people who don't have children or anyone to support them. There are no social benefits. They beg on the streets and often have nowhere to live.

Herman bought a large parcel of land and built the village on it (which Gillian and I visited), with medical and dental facilities, carers and helpers, etc. He has a minibus team which finds the elderly vulnerable people and brings them to his village where they can all live together as a community.

The residents are required to pay nothing but they do join in activities like growing vegetables, etc., for their own consumption—none are for sale.

The village consists largely of little houses, typically with 2 men and 2 women living in them as companions.

It is my belief that **this man, Herman, is a true Christian** and that some hypocrite who goes to church and sings a few hymns **is not necessarily a Christian!**

****

And so you see, I have long regarded myself as being something of a philanthropist.

****

Philanthropy

Some time ago, I found the modern definition of philanthropy in Wikipedia:

It means the love of humanity. The definition also serves to contrast philanthropy with business endeavours which are private initiatives for private good, **focusing on material gain** and with government endeavours which are (or should be) for public good, **focusing on public services.**

****

I feel very 'rewarded' and have a deep feeling of satisfaction from the knowledge that I have spent virtually my entire life working for the good of the community and the public benefit, rather than just working for what I call 'asshole companies' that are interested only in profit for private gain and don't hesitate to use people and sack people.

One of my pet hates is the managers of such companies I have encountered over the years.

The great majority of them are what I call 'chancers'. They have either 'blagged' their way into the job or have got there basically through the 'old school tie network'. Under scrutiny, you very often find they don't have much in the way of formal qualifications and tend to be less qualified than the people they manage.

They act as if they are 'the boss', when in fact they are nothing of the sort. They are employees, the same as their staff. They are power-struck and have lost sight of the fact that they are there to support their staff, not boss them around. So the bottom line is, they are not worth the money they are paid, rely on the knowledge and skills of the staff under them and are carried by them.

When it comes to job losses, they ensure they remain and get rid of some of the staff who are, in fact, more valuable than they are. Little better than leeches! Readers must have encountered some of them along the way.

****

I have never been a supporter of the idea that everything has to be run for private profit and I never will be.

That is all part of 'the system' which is designed to ensure that the privileged get richer at the expense of the poor. Capitalism and the monetarists ideas are sick in my opinion.

You have to think of everyone instead of just yourself.

Whilst children starve to death, there can never be a justification for some obscenely rich woman spending £60,000 on a handbag.

When I was born, we were coping with Hitler and Mussolini but I think it is actually worse now than then. We now have or have had the likes of Ceausescu, Gaddafi,

Saddam Hussein, Mugabe, Kim Jong Un, Erdogan, Assad and Putin. Corrupt and evil people!

We are in a world of dictators, despots, oligarchs, magnates, oil barons, drug barons and the like. Call them what you will, they are all the same.

They are greedy people who want to maintain corruption, disparity, etc., etc. so they can become even more obscenely rich and powerful.

Take a well-known Media and Airline tycoon for example. Allegedly, this man has millions already and he owns a private island. What is he doing at present? Allegedly, he is taking millions from our NHS in payments for parts of it he has cherry-picked and privatised. At the same time, he is allegedly suing the NHS for millions over contracts he has not won. How the hell does someone like that get knighted? Something is very, very wrong in a society that can allow that to happen!

Aneurin Bevan MP—the founder of our NHS, once said:

"The Tories always hold the view that the state is an apparatus for the protection of the property owners…Christ drove the money changers out of the temple, but you inscribe their title deed on the altar cloth."

He also said: "The purpose of getting power is to be able to give it away."

The only thing that globalisation, capitalism, privatisation and monetarism have brought us, is that our once great country is now essentially owned by and controlled by foreigners.

What a legacy to leave the children!

There was a time in history when anyone 'selling the family silver' (the nation's assets), would have been executed at the Tower of London. How fitting that would be for the likes of Thatcher, offshore money—Cameron and now May!

The architects of the 'greed-oriented society' that we all now live in.

But just look at the changes that have taken place, everyone now has cars, televisions, washing machines, cookers, fridges, etc., etc. Even the kids have their own cars! Everything has gone from austerity to excess!

****

Helen and I did not become a 'couple' and 11 years on we are still not 'a couple', we are companions. I was astonished when her sister Carol assumed we were a couple not long ago, whilst we were telling her of the very high cost of the Harley Street lady. Carol said: "Well, Ken will have to get an advance on the equity of the house."

I have written hundreds of letters for Helen, attended and won 2 Tribunals for her, taken her to countless appointments all over the place, attended to all her correspondences, got her a Passport because her ex-husband denied her an identity by keeping all her papers. After all these years, he has still not let Helen have copies of photographs of her children when they were young. He is a 'control freak' who gets some weird pleasure from withholding them from her.

I have paid all household and food bills without ever asking Helen for money towards any of them.

Some people are aware of much but not all of that which followed when I finally 'took Helen under my wing' so to speak.

I know that Mary (my wife's and Helen's mother), was very resentful of me taking away her Helen but the bottom line is that Helen was being unwittingly neglected.

I also know that some people had their suspicions about my motives but they were and are, for the purpose of trying to get her out of an awful mess and that was simply not going to happen without my intervention.

My motive and mission remain the same as it was on day one. I earnestly believe that if our dear Gillian is looking down upon us—she will approve of my efforts to help Helen over these last extremely difficult 15 years—because she and Helen were very close indeed.

Gillian and Helen

We saw the world together and I believe she still loves me
She wants me to live on now, wants me to be grief-free
I believe she's watching over us although we're now apart
Wants me to help her sister, I can feel it in my heart.
The two of them were very close, that is a simple fact
I know that there was no pretence, no putting on an act
When Helen picked up her telephone on 253601
Gillian said, "It's only me," and then they had some fun.
Helen had to answer questions to catch up on the TV soaps
It was like doing an exam and being 'on the ropes'
Often I'd pick up my extension phone when I was in my den
They'd say to me "Get off the line—we're not talking to you, Ken."
Through different circumstances and then losing their dear mother
We both had a steep hill to climb and had to help each other.
The hill has proved to be a high one, the top we can't yet see
Her children show a lack of support, don't act like family.
Helen also lost her little 'Gadget' dog, her one remaining love
But he's just over the rainbow in a better place above
She can no longer play with him and tease him with his ball

But I'm certain he still loves her because pure love conquers all.
We haven't finished climbing yet, there are still goals we must achieve
But we must keep on looking forward and not stand still and grieve
Because we're children of the universe and have a right to be here
So we must work hard and try to please Gillian because she's still so very dear.

By Ken, 15 February 2019

****

So, in a brief summary, I came from a poverty-stricken family, lost my dad, had to go to school at age 3, was denied an appropriate education because of my 'social class', was partially brought up by other family members. I was treated very badly by my first employer and decided to try to change things for all ordinary people.

At various times in my life, despite going 9 times 'under the knife' with spinal, knee, hip, hernia and prostate surgery, etc. and after losing £22,000 to my nephew builder, who didn't tell us he was bankrupt whilst building our house, I still managed to progress a bit further.

A quote which is apparently from *Mencius*, Book VI, ii 15. Circa 500 B.C.

"When heaven wishes to impose a great mission upon a man, it deems it proper at first to fill his heart with bitterness, to subject his nerves and his bones to weariness, to deliver his whole body to the torments of hunger, to reduce him and to exhaust him, frustrating and overthrowing all his undertakings. In this manner, it gives strength to his heart, endows his will with endurance; it increases him in stature and gives him the power to carry out that of which he would have been incapable."

My reward lies in the achievement of fighting my way out of all that went before and ending up being told by a Ministry of Defence Personnel Department that my qualifications are the equivalent of a degree.

I was presented with a handwritten valedictory letter by Sir Ian Vallance, the chairman of British Telecom in which he wrote to thank me for my contribution to the company. He also handed me a cheque for £500 and said, "Go and buy yourself a nice leaving present." I bought myself an Olympus Trip 35mm camera.

A Royal Navy Lieutenant Commander, who was in charge of their maritime communications, wrote me a reference to Taunton Deane Council and stated:

"I consider that if the M.O.D. let Ken go, they will be shooting themselves in the foot."

I won the friendship of Herman Theodorus Steur and Sir Arthur C. Clarke the philanthropists.

Strangely, they both told me basically the same thing. They liked my left-wing approach to the needs of this world of ours.

I believe I am entitled to say that I have contributed a little to humanity, through very hard times, through very hard work and endeavour and by helping others in their time of need.

Michael Jackson was a Virgo, the same as me. He constantly sought to change the world and tried to tell people in his music: "I can't do it by myself" and "I'm talking about The Man in the Mirror."

I once took Helen to meet with Michael's brother, Tito Jackson, in North Devon.

Whilst in Bucharest, Romania to do a concert, for example, Michael allegedly visited an appalling Children's Hospital. (I have visited them myself). Michael told the concert organisers, "I am paying and I want these hospitals sorted out, I will not appear in your concert unless I see action now."
John Lennon was opinionated in much the same way.

My own 'community first' beliefs are one of the underlying reasons why I went to Sri Lanka to help after the Tsunami.
The other reason was the fact that Gillian and I loved the place and its people. We had some wonderful friends there and I felt it was my duty to go and help them in their time of need. I also did it as a way of helping me to overcome my grief from losing Gillian. I saw it as a sort of pilgrimage.
I had difficulty getting anyone to come with me and ended up taking my French sister-in-law, Brigitte and Sir Arthur C. Clarke's brother, Fred, who was not able to travel alone. Fred and I met up with Brigitte at London Heathrow Airport. From there, the three of us flew to Colombo, Sri Lanka.

On arrival, the three of us stayed at the Galle Face Hotel in Colombo. It is a lovely old Colonial Hotel facing the green. In the foyer is a bust of Sir Arthur, who had written one of his books there and also a huge list of famous people who have also stayed there. We were given the best rooms over the entrance because they knew we were bringing Sir Arthur's brother.

The very same day we arrived, we had an invitation card put under the door of our hotel room. We were invited to a private cocktail party which the hotel arranged for us and about 4 or 5 others staying there.

After a few days there, Fred was able to go and stay with his brother Arthur whilst Brigitte and I embarked further afield. Before going, we consulted with Arthur and he passed us over to a lady called Valerie who was directly involved in Aid Work. She was the wife of a fellow called Hector Ekanaike. Hector ran Sir Arthur's SCUBA Diving Centres as a manager.

Valerie recommended that we meet up with and assist a German fellow named Stefan Birckmann who had been reviving the traditional Sri Lankan Puppets.

We stayed in Negombo and then at Hikkaduwa, where we met up with Stefan Birckmann.

We helped with orphaned and injured children in hospitals and orphanages. I have over 700 photos of some of the children, etc. Other things I did include helping to fund the revival of the traditional Sri Lankan giant puppets, **which could talk to the children and help them psychologically.**

Some of the puppets performing.

A captive audience! – Photo taken from backstage.

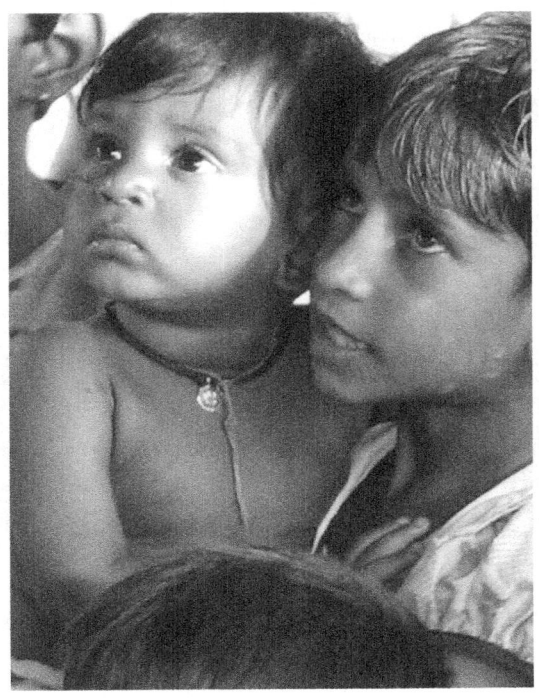

The little girl is 8 years old and apparently she is holding her baby sister. The 8-year-old has become a mum because their parents were apparently killed by the tsunami.

I helped fund this revival from my own money.

To give some idea of the value of money at that time, a typical hotel manager friend of mine in Sri Lanka was earning about £35.00 per month working long hours.

I gave American $1000.00 of my own money to the Puppets Revival Organiser (Stefan) and found it very rewarded by doing so.

During 2018, I again contacted Stefan Birckmann, a great German guy whom Brigitte and I met in Sri Lanka, on the recommendation of Sir Arthur. Stefan was the guy who actually did all the work of reviving the puppets.

Stefan, Brigitte and me whilst staying at the Reef Hotel, Hikkaduwa.

I was delighted to learn (in 2018) that the puppets are still going and that after my own contribution, UNICEF had stepped in to continue it. It is called the Saranga Puppet Society. UNICEF and those involved (including me), are known as 'Mango Friends' and I am told that I am an honorary life member.

I also came across a very talented young boy who was playing the violin and was stunned to discover his poor father was renting it to him. I took the boy and his father to Colombo in my minibus with driver, which I was hiring full time. I bought the boy a violin there and then took great pleasure in thrusting the rented one back into the hands of the person who was taking money for it.

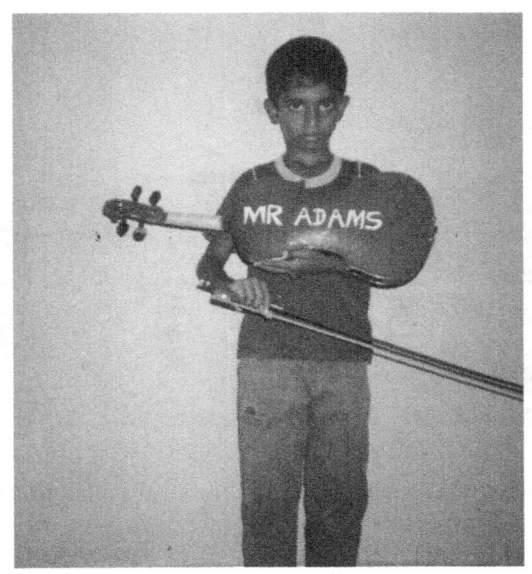

The boy and his violin.

Warning sign near Hikkaduwa.

This train was actually knocked off the rails onto its side at Hikkaduwa.

With Sir Arthur C. Clarke in his office at 'Leslie's House' in Barnes Place, Colombo.

At The Galle Face Hotel, Colombo. Sir Arthur's bust is in the background.

Fred and Brigitte being portered to the departure lounge at Heathrow Airport.

****

Finally, I have to say that I am deeply alarmed by the way we are destroying our planet by the removal and consumption of all its natural resources in the pursuit of ever more money for the greedy.

As I write (on 2 February 2023), we are experiencing an unprecedented number of strikes by our postmen, rail workers, nurses, teachers, etc.

In my opinion, all this disruption has been caused by years of privatisation, underfunding, pay cuts and inflation by the Tory government. All of our utilities have been sold off into private hands, our NHS is gradually being privatised, we have no British car manufacturers. Even British Steel is owned by foreigners.

We simply cannot allow our once proud nation to continue to be owned and controlled by foreign interests.

Ordinary workers are saying they have had enough of facing ever-higher bills from greedy companies who want ever-higher returns for their shareholders whilst seeing their own income falling all the time. They have to dutifully pay their taxes whilst seeing high earners dodging tax all the time through loopholes.

The government response is trying to introduce legislation to stop strikes! They simply cannot bring themselves to embrace the fact that they have to stop favouring the rich at the expense of the poor.

The big problem is ever-widening disparity.

It has now become very necessary to have the world's resources and finances under the control of ordinary people not under the exclusive control of the greedy few.

I know that many people will think I am living in a dream world, but I believe Great Britain needs to be re-established by taking back all of what was once public property into public ownership and out of the ownership of profit-driven companies.

I also believe we must prevent the break-up of Great Britain by the likes of Nicola Sturgeon, who seems obsessed with making Scotland independent. (Probably to further her own ends.)

She should be told in no uncertain terms that if they go independent, they will not be allowed to use Sterling as their currency. May I suggest they call their new currency the Scottish Kilt!

We were once described as a nation of shopkeepers and ironically, many of them dodge tax by not giving receipts and keeping two books for that purpose!

It's time to take back control!

I also believe that family values have deteriorated with the advent and huge growth of social media. People seem to think that they don't need to visit each other anymore!

Backwards Progress

I often saw my relatives or met up with my mates,
but what happens nowadays is one of my pet hates
Technology moves on apace but I am not the type,
to just settle for Facebook or Instagram or Skype
I have a mind of my own and don't live 'on a screen'
people should be together with nothing in between
Two folks living together, I saw hastening their doom,
when I saw them talk on Facebook, although in the same room

That money-grabbing media man has much to answer for,
their 'dark side' stock excuses just leave me on the floor
I look at my telephone and wonder why it never rings,
or look at some old photos and remember the good things
Families have split apart and gone their separate ways,
don't even see their children long grown-up from their plays
COVID is not the only reason why visiting is dead,
people now just get on with their lives and stay away instead
The weakness of the human race is greed and selfishness,
pursuing their indulgences and living in constant stress

They ought to get together more and forget things that cost money,
the very simple things in life are the real, elusive honey
Walk away from that computer and that cursed mobile phone,
and then start to remember that people are alone
Start by picking up the telephone and saying, "It's only me,"
then say "Let's get together and have a cup of tea."

By: Ken Adams, 31 July 2020

(Which would have been our 48th anniversary if my dear Gillian was still here.)

****

So now, I'll just conclude with a few of the words of a song by Michael Jackson:
"What about all the greed—Where did we go wrong?"
And John Lennon:
"Imagine."
And in his '1984 Spring' book, my friend Sir Arthur C. Clarke (no, not George Orwell) wrote:
"Upon us, the heirs to all the past and the trustees of a future which our folly can slay before its birth lies a responsibility no other age has ever known. If we fail in our generation, those who come after us may be too few to rebuild the world, when the dust of the cities has descended and the radiation of the rocks has died away."
I cite John Lennon again:

"You may say I'm a dreamer—but I'm not the only one."
Wake up, people, our very existence is under threat!

Ken Adams, February 2023

Made in the USA
Monee, IL
03 May 2026